小故事小智慧

Short Stories of Chinese Wisdom

The Commercial Press

Beginner **Read about China**

小故事小智慧

Short Stories of Chinese Wisdom

pearlchoy@gmail.com

First Edition, February 2012

Published by:
The Commercial Press (U.S.) Ltd.
The Corporation, 2nd Floor
New York, NY 10013

Short Stories of Chinese Wisdom
Beginner Readings in Language and Culture

Author: Feng Mengqi
Editor: Edmond Hung

ISBN: 978 962 07 1956 1
Printed in Hong Kong

http://www.chinese4fun.net

Contents
目　录

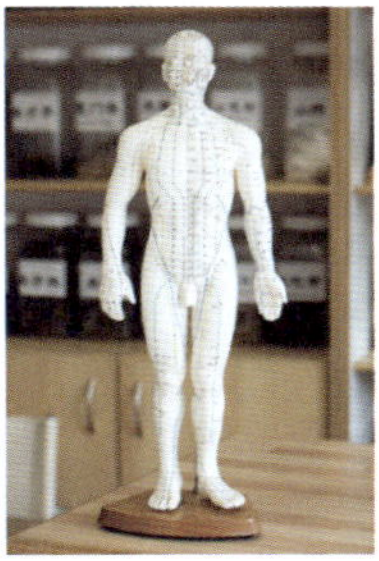

出版说明　Publisher's Note

一、　中医的智慧
The wisdom of Chinese medicine

1. 不给病人吃药的大夫 1
Treating a patient without medicine

2. 大夫给的药 3
Medicine from a physician

Expansion Reading　How Chinese medicine works

GAMES FOR FUN

二、　劳动中的发现
Discoveries made at work

1. 鲁班与锯 8
Lu Ban and the saw

2. 写“一”字 10
Writing the “yi” character

Expansion Reading Innovations created through labor

GAMES FOR FUN

三、 聪明的将军
Wise generals

1. 有用的小偷 16
A useful thief

2. 梅子的作用 18
The effect of plums

Expansion Reading Using a small army to overcome a large one

四、 厨师只会做菜吗
Chefs do more than just cook

1. 肉上的头发 23
The hair on the meat

2. 一条腿的鸭子 25
A one-legged duck

Expansion Reading Wisdom in food

GAMES FOR FUN

五、 少年也有大智慧
Young in age, big on wisdom

1. 跳舞的鸡 30
The dancing chicken

2. 树在口中 32
A tree in a square

Expansion Reading Outstanding youths

GAMES FOR FUN

六、 怎样管理好国家
How to govern a nation

1. 节约的国王 36
The frugal emperor

2. 桃子和将军 38
Peaches and generals

Expansion Reading Wise emperors

七、 好的管理
An enlightened governance

1. 国王的晚会 43
The king's evening party

2. 死马换好马 45
Trading a dead horse for a good horse

Expansion Reading To value talents and use them wisely

八、 做个聪明的人
To be a wise person

1. 保护自己 51
Protecting oneself

2. 计算 53
To be calculating

Expansion Reading The Chinese who know how to protect themselves

九、 教育的方法
Tips on teaching

1. 孙武训练军人 58
Sun Wu trains his troops

2. 三次搬家的母亲 60
The mother who moved house three times

Expansion Reading The Chinese way of teaching and learning

GAMES FOR FUN

十、 生活的智慧
Wisdom in everyday life

1. 把牛叫做"爸爸" 65
Calling an ox "father"

2. 放下 66
Learning to let go

Expansion Reading Folk sayings: Documenting the wisdom of everyday life

GAMES FOR FUN

十一、不一样的学习
A different approach to learning

1. 射箭 72
Shooting an arrow

2. 黑带的真正意义 74
The true meaning of a black belt

Expansion Reading Is it really useful to be do well in school?

GAMES FOR FUN

十二、中国古代的智慧
Ancient Chinese wisdom

1. 不记住别人的错误 79
Do not remember the faults of others

2. 对与错 81
Of right and wrong

Expansion Reading Traditional virtues of China

Glossary 87

PUBLISHER'S NOTE

After studying one to two years of Chinese you have also gained the knowledge of quite a bit of vocabulary. You may be wondering whether there are any other ways for you to further improve your Chinese language proficiency? Although there are a lot of books in the market that are written for people who are studying Chinese it is not easy to find an interesting and easy to read book that matches up to one's level of proficiency. You may find the content and the choice of words for some books to be too difficult to handle. You may also find some books to be too easy and the content is too naive for high school students and adults. Seeing the demand for this kind of learning materials we have designed a series of reading materials, which are composed of vivid and interesting content, presented in a multi-facet format. We think this can help students who are learning Chinese to solve the above problem. Through our reading series you can improve your Chinese and at the same time you will learn a lot of Chinese culture.

Our series includes Chinese culture, social aspects of China, famous Chinese literary excerpts, pictorial symbols of China, famous Chinese heroes...and many other indispensable aspects of China for those who want to really understand Chinese culture. While enjoying the reading materials one can further one's knowledge of Chinese culture from different angles. The content of the series are contextualized according to the wordbase categorization of The content of the series are contextualized according to the word base categorization of HSK and GCS. We have selected our diction from the elementary, beginner, intermediate to advanced level of Chinese language learners. Our series is suitable for students at the pre-intermediate, intermediate to advanced level of Chinese and working people who are studying Chinese on their own.

The body of our series is composed of literary articles. The terms used in each article are illustrated with the romanised system called Hànyǔ pīnyīn for the ease in learning the pronunciation. Each article has an English translation with explanation of the vocabulary. Moreover there is related background knowledge in Expansion Reading. Interesting games are added to make it fun to learn. We aim at presenting a three-dimensional study experience of learning Chinese for our readers.

Zhōngyī de zhìhuì

中医的智慧

The wisdom of Chinese medicine

Pre-reading Questions

1. What impression do you have of Chinese medicine?
2. Have you or any of your family and friends ever tried Chinese medicine? How effective was it?

Bù gěi bìngrén chī yào de dàifu

❶ 不给病人吃药的大夫

Cóngqián, yǒu yī gè guānyuán bìng le hěn jiǔ, chī guo hěn duō yào yě méiyǒu hǎo qilai. Tā jiù zhǎo yī gè hěn yǒumíng de dàifu kànbìng.

从前，有一个官员病了很久，吃过很多药也没有好起来。他就找一个很有名的大夫看病。

Dàifu kàn guo hòu, zhīdao zhège guānyuán shēngbìng shì yīnwèi xīnli bù kuàile, jiù xiǎng chu le yī gè zhìbìng de bànfǎ.

大夫看过后，知道这个官员生病是因为心里不快乐，就想出了一个治病的办法。

Tā xiàng guānyuán yào le hěn duō qián shuō gěi tā zhìbìng
他向官员要了很多钱，说给他治病
yòng de Kěshì dàifu shōu le qián méiyǒu liúxia yào jiù
用的。可是，大夫收了钱，没有留下药就
zǒu le Tā hái liúxia yī fēng xìn shuō le hěn duō bù
走了。他还留下一封信，说了很多不
hǎo de huà
好的话。

Guānyuán shífēn shēngqì yào érzi bǎ dàifu zhuā
官员十分生气，要儿子把大夫抓
huilai
回来。

Dàifu bèi zhuā hòu shuō chu le tā zhèyàng zuò de
大夫被抓后，说出了他这样做的
yuányīn Guānyuán de érzi míngbai dàifu zhèyàng zuò shì
原因。官员的儿子明白大夫这样做是
wèile zhì hǎo fùqīn de bìng jiù bǎ tā fàng le
为了治好父亲的病，就把他放了。

Guānyuán tīngshuō érzi bǎ dàifu fàngzǒu mǎshàng qì de
官员听说儿子把大夫放走，马上气得
tù chu le yī kǒu hēi xiě Rénmen yǐwéi tā de bìng yīdìng
吐出了一口黑血。人们以为他的病一定
biàn de gèng zhòng
变得更重。

Kěshì guò le
可是，过了
bùjiǔ tā de
不久，他的
bìng jiù hǎo le
病就好了。

Zhōngyī jiùshì
中医就是

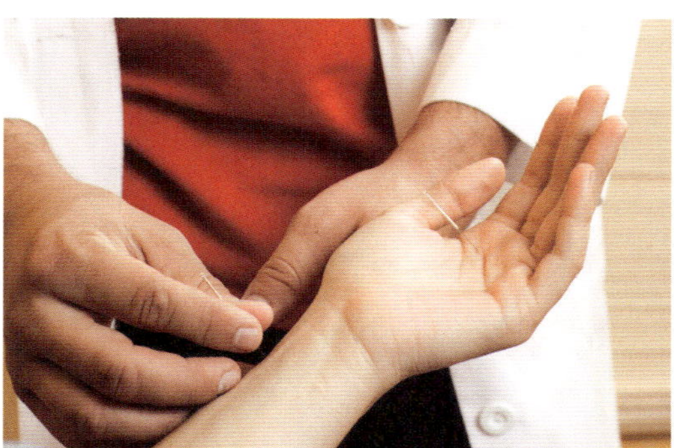
A Chinese physician checking a patient's pulse

zhèyàng zhìbìng bù yīdìng yào kào chīyào Zhǐyào zhǎodào
这样，治病不一定要靠吃药。只要找到

shēngbìng de yuányīn jiù kěyǐ lìyòng gèzhǒng zìrán de
生病的原因，就可以利用各种自然的

tiáojiàn qù bǎ bìng zhì hǎo
条件去把病治好。

❷ 大夫给的药

Dàifu gěi de yào

Yī gè dàifu gěi yī gè lǎorén hé yī gè xiǎohái
一个大夫给一个老人和一个小孩

kànbìng hou bǎ yào jiāogěi le tāmen
看病后，把药交给了他们。

Bìngrén zǒu hou yī gè xuésheng wèn dàifu
病人走后，一个学生问大夫：

Lǎoshī zhè liǎng gè rén de bìng yīyàng wèishénme nín gěi
“老师，这两个人的病一样，为什么您给

lǎorén de yào shǎo yīxiē gěi xiǎohái de yào duō yīxiē
老人的药少一些，给小孩的药多一些

ne
呢？”

Dàifu xiào zhe shuō Nàge lǎorén yǐjing hěn lǎo
大夫笑着说：“那个老人已经很老

le tā hěn xiǎng zìjǐ de bìng zǎo diǎn hǎo qilai
了，他很想自己的病早点好起来。

Suǒyǐ tā huíjiā hòu yīdìng chīyào Yěxǔ hái huì duō chī
所以，他回家后一定吃药。也许还会多吃

yīxiē suǒyǐ gěi tā de yào yào shǎo yīdiǎn
一些，所以给他的药要少一点。”

Nàge xiǎohái yīnwèi shēngbìng zǒngshì kū yòu bù
“那个小孩因为生病总是哭，又不

xiǎng chīyào Dàrén ràng tā chī de yào yīdìng huì làngfèi
想吃药。大人让他吃的药，一定会浪费

bù shǎo. Suǒyǐ
不少。所以
wǒ zhǐhǎo duō
我只好多
gěi tā yīdiǎnr
给他一点儿
yào. Bù zhèyàng
药。不这样
zuò, xiǎohái de
做，小孩的

Chinese herbal medicine

bìng shì méifǎ hǎo qilai de
病是没法好起来的。”

Nǐ yào jìzhu shí gè bìngrén jiù yǒu shí zhǒng
“你要记住，十个病人就有十种
bùtóng de qíngkuàng wǒmen bù néng tóngyàng duìdài a
不同的情况，我们不能同样对待啊！”

Rénmen dōu yǐwéi dàrén yòng de yào yào duō xiǎohái
人们都以为大人用的药要多，小孩
yòng de yào yào shǎo Kěshì zài zhōngyī kànlai gēnjù
用的药要少。可是，在中医看来，根据
bìngrén de shíjì qíngkuàng yòngyào cáishì zuì yǒuxiào de
病人的实际情况用药，才是最有效的。

Translation

❶ Treating a patient without medicine

A long time ago, an official was ill for a long time, and he did not get better despite taking plenty of medicine. He sought the help of a famous physician.

The physician saw the official, and found that he was ill because he was not happy. And so the physician thought of a way to cure him.

The physician asked the official for a lot of money, saying that this was needed to treat his illness. But, after taking the money, the physician left without leaving any medicine. He even left a note with many unpleasant words on it.

The official was furious, and got his son to arrest the physician. After the physician was seized, he revealed the reason behind his actions. The official's son realized that the physician did all this to cure his father, and so he let the physician go.

When the official learnt that his son let the physician go, he got so angry that he spewed black blood. People thought the official's condition had become worse. But he recovered from his illness soon after.

In Chinese medicine, it is not always necessary to rely on medicine to cure illnesses. So long as the root of the illness can be found, various ways can be used to cure it in a natural manner.

❷ Medicine from a physician

A physician had just finished seeing an old man and a boy, and passed them their medicine.

After the patients had left, a student asked the physician: "Teacher, those two patients have the same illness. Why did you give less medicine to the old man but more medicine to the boy?"

The physician said with a smile: "The old man is already advanced in age, and he wants to be cured as soon as possible. So he will take his medicine the moment he gets home. He may even take a bit more than he should. That is why I gave him less medicine.

"The boy cries a lot because he is ill, and does not want to take his medicine. When people try to feed him, there is bound to be quite a lot of medicine wasted. That is why I had to give him more medicine. If that were not done, the boy's illness will not be cured.

"Remember, ten patients mean ten different situations to deal with. We cannot treat them all the same way!"

People commonly assume that adults will need more medicine, while children need less medicine. However, in Chinese medicine, it is far more effective to prescribe medicine based on each patient's actual condition.

Expansion Reading

How Chinese medicine works

Chinese medicine and Western medicine are fundamentally different in their theoretical principles.

Chinese medicine views human beings as part of the natural world. Under normal conditions, the human body adapts to changes in nature, and is in a dynamic state of balance. When this dynamic equilibrium is disrupted, a person will fall ill.

Chinese physicians diagnose a patient's condition based on examination of four characteristics. They will examine the patient's outward appearance and complexion, feel the patient's pulse, ask the patient about the symptoms of the illness, and listen to the voice and sounds from the patient.

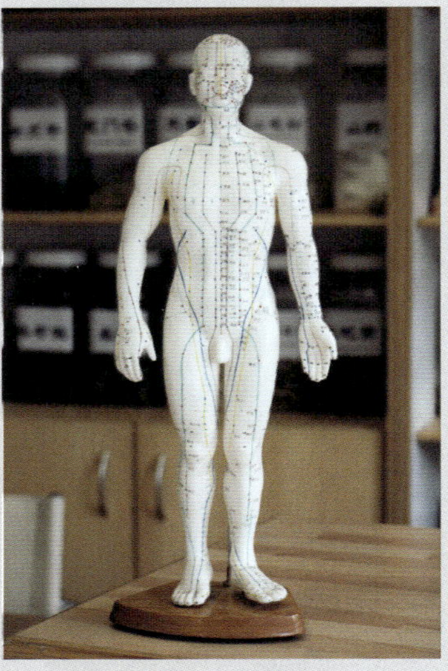
Map of acupuncture points on the human body

When treating illnesses, Chinese medicine emphasizes a holistic and balanced treatment. It also emphasizes taking appropriate measures based on current circumstances, local situation and the individual's condition. Treatment methods can be different even for the same illness. This is because every person has a unique physique and condition.

Moreover, Chinese medicine views life rhythms and illnesses as being intimately linked to changes in the natural world. The differences in the natural environment that people live in, and differences in how people adapt to the natural environment, will lead to differences in physical characteristics and incidence of illnesses.

GAMES FOR FUN

See if you can tell what scenarios are represented by these pictures. Which of these are unique to Chinese medicine?

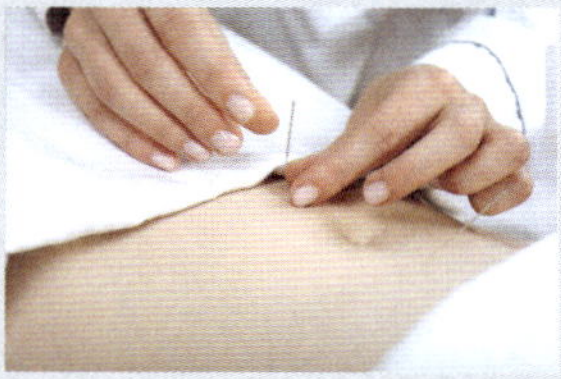

(a)

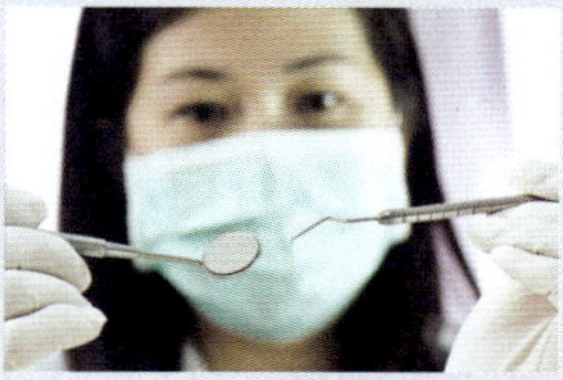

(b)

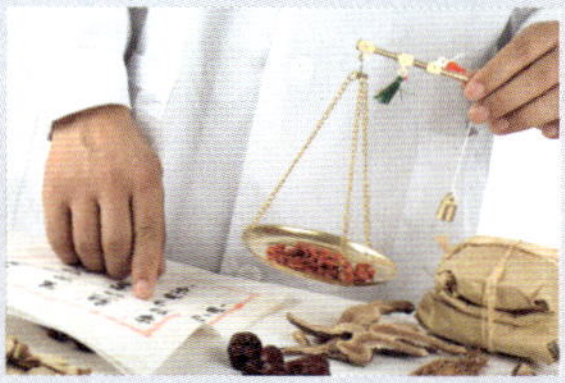

(c)

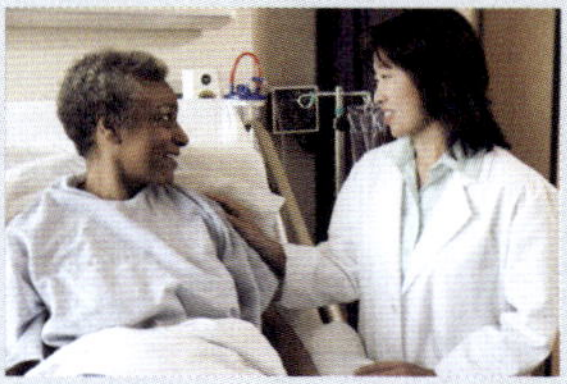

(d)

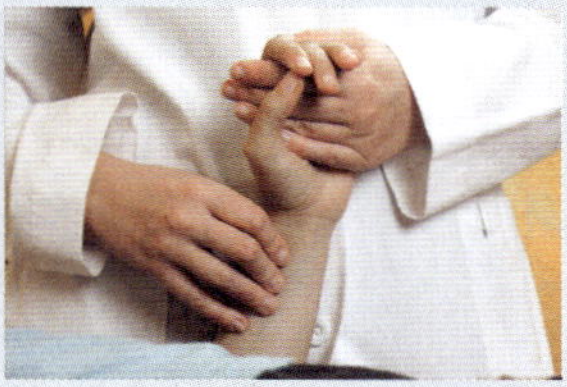

(e)

Answer: A, C, E

Láodòng zhōng de fāxiàn

劳动中的发现

Discoveries made at work

Pre-reading Questions

1. Have you ever heard of the four great inventions of ancient China? Can you name two of them?
2. Have you ever used a saw? How do you think the invention of the saw has benefited us?

Lǔ Bān yǔ jù

❶ 鲁 班 与 锯

Lǔ Bān zài Zhōngguó gǔdài hěn yǒumíng. Tā zào de

鲁 班 在 中国 古代 很 有名。他 造 的

A leaf with serrated edges

gōngjù, tā jiàn de fángzi, dōu fēicháng hǎo.

工具，他 建 的 房子，都 非常 好。

Yǒu yī cì, Lǔ Bān yào zài

有 一 次，鲁 班 要 在

hěn duǎn de shíjiān li, jiàn yī zuò gāolóu.
很短的时间里，建一座高楼。

Lǔ Bān dài zhe xuésheng dào shānshang, zhǎo jiàn gāolóu de cáiliào.
鲁班带着学生到山上，找建高楼的材料。

Yóuyú tāmen yòng de gōngjù hěn chà, suīrán měitiān hěn zǎo jiù qǐlai gōngzuò, háishi bù néng jíshí bǎ cáiliào yùn dào chéngli. Lǔ Bān xīnli hěn zháojí.
由于他们用的工具很差，虽然每天很早就起来工作，还是不能及时把材料运到城里。鲁班心里很着急。

Yǒu yī tiān, tā zài shùlín li gōngzuò, bù xiǎoxīn bèi yī zhǒng cǎo nòng shāng le shǒu.
有一天，他在树林里工作，不小心被一种草弄伤了手。

Tā bǎ cǎo lā guolai yī kàn, fāxiàn cǎo de biān zhǎng de xiàng yáchǐ yīyàng. Shǒu jīngguò cǎo de biānshang, hěn róngyì jiù huì shòushāng.
他把草拉过来一看，发现草的边长得像牙齿一样。手经过草的边上，很容易就会受伤。

Zhèshíhou, yī zhī chóngzi fēi guolai, luò zài cǎoshang zhǎo shíwù. Lǔ Bān kànjian nà zhī chóngzi chī cǎo de shíhou, yě shì yòng yáchǐ, chī de hěn kuài.
这时候，一只虫子飞过来，落在草上找食物。鲁班看见那只虫子吃草的时候，也是用牙齿，吃得很快。

Lǔ Bān mǎshàng xiǎngdào: Rúguǒ bǎ gōngjù zuò chéng yáchǐ de yàngzi, nàme gōngzuò de sùdù yīdìng huì kuài
鲁班马上想到：如果把工具做成牙齿的样子，那么工作的速度一定会快

hěn duō
很多！

Tā bǎ xuésheng jiào lái bǎ xiǎngfǎ gàosu tāmen
他把学生叫来，把想法告诉他们。Hěn kuài xuéshengmen jiù zhào zhe cǎo de yàngzi yòng zhúzi
很快，学生们就照着草的样子，用竹子zào chu yī zhǒng gōngjù Tāmen fāxiàn zhèzhǒng gōngjù hěn
造出一种工具。他们发现，这种工具很róngyì jiù bǎ shùpí nòng pò Bùguò tā hěn kuài jiù duàn
容易就把树皮弄破。不过，它很快就断le bù néng zài yòng
了，不能再用。

Kěshì Lǔ Bān hěn gāoxìng tā ràng xuésheng zhào zhège
可是鲁班很高兴，他让学生照这个yàngzi yòng tiě chóngxīn zuò le yī bǎ Yòng le zhèzhǒng
样子用铁重新做了一把。用了这种gōngjù yǐhòu gōngzuò de sùdù guǒrán tígāo le Lǔ Bān
工具以后，工作的速度果然提高了。鲁班hé tā de xuéshengmen zuìhòu yě wánchéng le rènwu
和他的学生们最后也完成了任务。

Zhèzhǒng gōngjù jiùshì jùzi
这种工具就是锯子。

Xiě yī zì
❷ 写“一”字

Gǔshíhou yī gè guówáng yào bǎ Chángchéng chóngxīn
古时候，一个国王要把长城重新xiūhǎo
修好。

Chángchéngshang yǒu yī zuò dàlóu jiàozuò
长城上有一座大楼，叫做tiānxiàdì-yīguān Qízhōng de yī zì diào le xiàlái
“天下第一关”。其中的“一”字掉了下来，

guówáng zhǎo rén chóngxīn xiě shangqu
国王找人重新写上去。

Hěn duō xiězì hěn hǎo de rén, dōu lái xiě zhège
很多写字很好的人，都来写这个

yī zì kěshì guówáng dōu bù mǎnyì
“一”字，可是国王都不满意。

Yǒu yī gè niánqīngrén shuō tā yě yào lái shìshi
有一个年轻人，说他也要来试试。

Dàjiā dōu shuō Nàme duō rén dōu xiě bù hǎo nǐ
大家都说：“那么多人都写不好，你

zhème niánqīng kěndìng yě xiě bù hǎo
这么年轻，肯定也写不好。”

Méi xiǎngdào niánqīngrén xiě de yī zì jiù gēn
没想到，年轻人写的“一”字，就跟

yuánlái de yī wánquán yīyàng
原来的“一”完全一样。

Dàjiā dōu bù míngbai wèishénme
大家都不明白为什么。

Niánqīngrén shuō Wǒ
年轻人说：“我

tiāntiān zài zhè zuò lóu xià
天天在这座楼下

gànhuó gàn le shí duō nián
干活，干了十多年

le Gànhuó de shíhou wǒ jiù
了。干活的时候我就

kàn zhe zhège yī zì
看着这个‘一’字，

hái jīngcháng yòng bǐ qù huà
还经常用笔去画。

Xiànzài wǒ zhǐshì bǎ tā
现在，我只是把它

The Great Wall

zài huà chulai
再画出来。”

Zhège gùshi gàosu wǒmen Bùduàn liànxí cái néng
这个故事告诉我们：不断练习，才能

zhǎngwò zuòhǎo shìqing de fāngfǎ
掌握做好事情的方法。

Translation

❶ Lu Ban and the saw

Lu Ban was a famous figure in ancient China. The tools he made and the houses he built were all excellent.

There was one time when Lu needed to construct a tall building in a short time.

Lu took his students to the mountains to find materials for constructing the building.

Because the tools they used were poor, they were unable to get the materials to the city in good time, despite starting work early every day.

Lu was feeling anxious.

As he was working in the woods his hand was accidentally hurt by a certain kind of grass.

He examined the grass and found that its edge was serrated, like teeth. It was easy to get hurt simply by brushing a hand lightly over the grass.

Just then, an insect flew over and landed on the grass in search of food. Lu saw that the insect was eating the grass with its teeth, and it was eating fast.

Lu immediately thought: If we could make a tool with teeth, that would make our work go a lot faster!

He called his students over and told them his idea. Soon his students used bamboo to make a tool based on the grass. They found that their tool could easily cut through the bark of a tree. But the tool broke straight away, and could not be used after that.

However, Lu was delighted. He got his students to make the same tool out of iron. With this tool, they indeed managed to work faster. Lu and his students were also able to finish their task on time.

This tool was the saw.

❷ Writing the " *yi* "character

A long time ago, an emperor wanted to restore the Great Wall. There was a tower on the Great Wall labeled "The First Pass Under Heaven". One of the characters, " *yi* ", had fallen off, and the emperor was looking for someone to replace it.

There were many people who could write very well, and they came to offer to write this " *yi* " character, but the emperor was not satisfied with what they wrote.

A young man said he wanted to give it a try. Everyone said: "So many people have tried and failed. You are so young, there's no way you can write it properly."

To everyone's surprise, the character " *yi* " that the young man wrote looked exactly the same as the original one.

No one could understand why.

The young man said: "I have been working at this tower for more than ten years. While working, I would look at this "*yi*" character, and often copy it with a brush. Now, I am simply repeating it again."

This story tells us: One must constantly practice in order to do something well.

Innovations created through labor

A bridge built entirely of stone

China has a history of more than two thousand years. During these two millenia, the early people were continuously gaining experience through their labors, and they created many admirable things.

During the Qin Dynasty, more than two thousand years ago, the Chinese people built the Dujiangyan Irrigation System near the city of Chengdu in Sichuan province. The project made use of the natural ecology and environment, and scientifically resolved the flow channel, deposition, volume of flow and other issues, eliminating flooding in the region around Chengdu. This project continues to play an important role today, and is one of the oldest surviving irrigation works in the world.

Craftsmen in ancient China had mastered advanced construction techniques as well. Some of the halls in Beijing's Forbidden City were constructed without using a single nail. Instead, the builders used a system of interlocking joints that was unique to China, andwhich has been effective enough to support the massive halls.

As early as the Han Dynasty (around two thousand years ago), China was alreadyusing a calculating machine. That was the abacus. The abacus could perform mathematical operations such as addition, subtraction, multiplication, division and solving square roots. It later spread to Japan, India, America and other places. This was an important milestone in the history of calculating machines. The abacus is still used by many people today.

GAMES FOR FUN

These ancient tools have the same functions as some modern tools. Can you guess which modern tools these are?

(1)

(a)

(2)

(b)

(3)

(c)

(4)

(d)

Answer: 1—C, 2—B, 3—D, 4—A

Cōngming de jiāngjūn

聪明的将军

Wise generals

Pre-reading Questions

1. Think of your friends. Are there any with special skills who could perhaps help you in future?
2. Besides plums, do you know of any other fruit that is effective in quenching thirst?

Yǒuyòng de xiǎotōu

❶ 有用 的 小偷

Cóngqián yǒu yī gè jiāngjūn jiāo le hěn duō péngyou
从前，有 一 个 将军，交 了 很 多 朋友。

zhèxiē rén dōu hěn yǒu nénglì
这些 人 都 很 有 能力。

Yǒu yī cì jiāngjūn yào hé biéguó de jūnduì zuòzhàn
有 一 次，将军 要 和 别国 的 军队 作战。

Yóuyú liǎngfāng shílì hěn jiējìn jiāngjūn yīzhí méiyǒu qǔdé shènglì
由于 两方 实力 很 接近，将军 一直 没有 取得 胜利。

Dāng tā jí de tuántuánzhuàn de shíhou yī gè dāng
当 他 急 得 团团转 的 时候，一 个 当

xiǎotōu de péngyou láidào jiāngjūn miànqián shuō Ràng wǒ lái
小偷的朋友来到将军面前，说：“让我来
bāng nǐ ba
帮你吧！”。

Zhè yī tiān wǎnshang xiǎotōu jìnrù duìfāng de dìfang
这一天晚上，小偷进入对方的地方，
bǎ duìfāng jiāngjūn de bēizi tōu le huílái Dào le
把对方将军的杯子偷了回来。到了
zǎoshang bǎ bēizi huán gěi duìfāng
早上，把杯子还给对方。

Dì-èr tiān wǎnshang xiǎotōu bǎ duìfāng jiāngjūn de yī
第二天晚上，小偷把对方将军的一
tào yīfu tōu le huílái Dào le zǎoshang yòu bǎ zhè tào
套衣服偷了回来。到了早上，又把这套
yīfu huán huiqu
衣服还回去。

Dì-sān tiān wǎnshang xiǎotōu bǎ duìfāng jiāngjūn tóushang de
第三天晚上，小偷把对方将军头上的
dōngxi tōu huilai ránhòu yòu
东西偷回来，然后又
yī cì sòng huiqu
一次送回去。

Zhèshíhou duìfāng de
这时候，对方的
jiāngjūn hàipà le Tā xīnli
将军害怕了。他心里
xiǎng Zài zhèyàng xiàqu
想：“再这样下去，
wǒ de tóu yīdìng bǎo bu
我的头一定保不
zhù
住。”

Statue of a Chinese general

Kěshì tā xiǎng le hěn jiǔ, zǒngshì zhǎo bù dào
可是，他 想 了 很 久，总是 找 不 到

bùràng duìfāng tōuzǒu dōngxi de bànfǎ, zhǐhǎo dài zhe
不让 对方 偷走 东西 的 办法，只好 带 着

jūnduì líkāi le.
军队 离开 了。

Měi gè rén dōu yǒu zìjǐ de chángchu. Fùzé guǎnlǐ
每 个 人 都 有 自己 的 长处。负责 管理

de rén, zhǐyào dǒngde lìyòng zhèxiē rén de chángchu, jiù
的 人，只要 懂得 利用 这些 人 的 长处，就

néng bǎ gōngzuò zuòhǎo.
能 把 工作 做好。

❷ Méizi de zuòyòng
梅子 的 作用

Cáo Cāo shì Zhōngguó gǔdài yī gè yǒumíng de jiāngjūn.
曹 操 是 中国 古代 一 个 有名 的 将军。

Yǒu yī cì, tā yào dài jūnduì gǎn qù yī gè zhànchǎng.
有 一 次，他 要 带 军队 赶 去 一 个 战场。

Tāmen zǒu le hěn jiǔ, zài yī gè shānbiān tíng le
他们 走 了 很 久，在 一 个 山边 停 了

xiàlái.
下来。

Zhèshíhou, yángguāng hěn hǎo, tiānqì hěn rè. Jūnduì
这时候，阳光 很 好，天气 很 热。军队

zhōng měi gè rén dōu hěn
中 每 个 人 都 很

lèi, yě hěn kě, dōu bù
累，也 很 渴，都 不

xiǎng zài zǒu le.
想 再 走 了。

Cáo Cāo wèn dàilù
曹 操 问 带路

Ripe plums on the tree

de rén Wǒmen néng zhǎodào shuǐ ma
的人："我们能找到水吗？"

Dàilù de rén shuō Zhèlǐ shì méiyǒu shuǐ de
带路的人说："这里是没有水的。"

Cáo Cāo kàndào hěnyuǎn hěnyuǎn de dìfang hǎoxiàng yǒu yī
曹操看到很远很远的地方，好像有一
piàn shùlín Tā tūrán dàshēng hǎn Wǒ xiǎng qilai le
片树林。他突然大声喊："我想起来了，
qiánmian bù yuǎn jiù yǒu yī piàn méizi shùlín nàli de
前面不远就有一片梅子树林，那里的
méizi yòudàyòutián Wǒmen xiàngzhe qiánmian zǒu ba hěn kuài
梅子又大又甜。我们向着前面走吧，很快
jiù dào le
就到了！"

Dàjiā tīngdào jiāngjūn zhèyàng shuō dōu hěn kāixīn
大家听到将军这样说，都很开心。
Xiǎngdào yòudàyòutián de méizi kǒuli hěn zìrán de yǒu
想到又大又甜的梅子，口里很自然地有
shuǐ liú xialai
水流下来。

Tāmen zǒu de hěn jí bújiǔ jiù zǒuchu le zhège
他们走得很急，不久就走出了这个
méiyǒu shuǐ de dìfang
没有水的地方。

Zhǐyào néng zhǎodào yī gè hǎo de fāngfǎ ràng
只要能找到一个好的方法，让
dàjiā de xīnzhōng yǒu le xīwàng zuòshì jiù bǐjiào róngyì
大家的心中有了希望，做事就比较容易
chénggōng
成功。

Translation

❶ A useful thief

A long time ago, there was a general who had many friends. All of them were capable people in their own way.

On one occasion, the general was fighting the army of another nation. Because both sides were closely matched in strength, the general was unable to achieve victory.

The general was feeling anxious. One of his friends was a thief, and he came to the general and said: "Let me help you!"

That night, the thief sneaked into the enemy's camp and stole the cup belonging to the enemy general. He returned the cup the next morning.

On the second night, the thief stole a set of the enemy general's clothes. He returned the clothes the next morning.

On the third night, the thief stole the headgear of the enemy general, and then returned it to him.

By now the enemy general was afraid. He thought: If this goes on, I will surely not be able to keep my own head.

Even after much thinking, he was unable to find a way to stop the rival side from stealing his things. And so he gathered his army and left.

Everybody has their strengths. A leader who knows how to harness people's strengths is one who can get the job done well.

❷ The effect of plums

Cao Cao was a famous general in ancient China. On one occasion, he was leading his army to the battlefield.

After walking for a long time, they stopped by the side of a mountain.

That day, the sun was strong and the weather was hot. Everyone in the army was tired and thirsty, and did not want to walk any further.

Cao Cao asked his guide: "Can we find water?"

The guide said: "There is no water here."

In the distance Cao Cao could see what looked like a forest. He suddenly yelled: "I remember now, there is a forest of plum trees not far ahead of us, and the plums there are big and sweet. Let's push on, we're almost there!"

When everyone heard these words from the general, they were delighted. The thought of big sweet plums made them drool.

They walked hurriedly, and soon they got out of the place without water.

So long as one can find a good solution that fills everyone's hearts with hope, it is easier for one to succeed.

Expansion Reading

Using a small army to overcome a large one

In the military history of China, there were many famous battles where a small army managed to defeat a larger one. These battles fully demonstrate the military intelligence of the commanders. For example, the famous general Cao Cao was once defeated in an important battle

The Yangtze River

by forces that were far smaller than his. That was the Battle of Chibi.
In the Battle of Chibi, Cao Cao's 200,000-strong army had set up camp on the Yangtze River, while the combined armies of the states of Wu and Shu numbered only 50,000. Cao's troops came from the north, and were used to fighting on flat land. As his troops were not used to living on ships, as well as fighting on water, Cao had his warships connected together to provide his troops and horses a flat platform to walk on. This move made things easier for Cao's army, but to the combined army of Wu and Shu, this was a fatal flaw for Cao.
The combined Wu and Shu army wrote a letter to Cao and pretended to surrender, so that they would have a chance to get close to Cao's warships. They sentsmall shipsthat were packed with flammable material towards Cao's warships. When the small ships were near Cao's warships, the combined army took advantage of the prevailing wind to use fire as a strategic weapon. They fired lighted arrows and ignited the small ships.. The wind made the flames burn fiercely, and in the end many of Cao's warships were destroyed, and many of his troops and horses were drowned. Then, the combined army, which had lain in ambush on the shore, launched a coordinated attack on Cao's army. Cao had no choice but to flee in retreat.
This victory established the tripartite arrangement of the Three Kingdoms, and the battle is still lauded to this day.

Chúshī zhǐhuì zuòcài ma

厨师只会做菜吗

Chefs do more than just cook

Pre-reading Questions

1. If you were dining outside, and there was a strand of hair on your food, what would you do?
2. When your family members prepare food for you, do you say anything to thank them? Why?

Ròushang de tóufa

❶ 肉上 的 头发

Cóngqián yǒu yī gè guówáng hěn ài chī ròu
从前，有 一 个 国王 很 爱 吃 肉。

Yǒu yī tiān guówáng chī ròu de shíhou fāxiàn ròushang yǒu yī tiáo tóufa Tā hěn shēngqì bǎ chúshī jiàolai wèn tā wèishénme fāshēng zhèyàng de shì
有 一 天，国王 吃 肉 的 时候，发现 肉上 有 一 条 头发。他 很 生气，把 厨师 叫来，问 他 为什么 发生 这样 的 事。

Chúshī liánmáng chéngrèn zìjǐ zuò de bù duì hái shuō zìjǐ zuòcuò le sān jiàn shì
厨师 连忙 承认 自己 做 得 不 对，还 说 自己 做错 了 三 件 事。

Guówáng gǎndào qíguài, jiù wèn: "Nǐ zuò cuò le nǎ sān jiàn shì ne?"
国王感到奇怪，就问："你做错了哪三件事呢？"

Chúshī shuō: "Dì-yī, wǒ de dāo méiyǒu nòng duàn zhè tiáo tóufa; dì-èr, wǒ bǎ ròu xǐ gānjìng fàng zài guō li, méiyǒu fāxiàn zhè tiáo tóufa; dì-sān, wǒ zuò cài de shíhou, huǒ nàme dà, zhè tiáo tóufa réngrán liú le xiàlái."
厨师说："第一，我的刀没有弄断这条头发；第二，我把肉洗干净放在锅里，没有发现这条头发；第三，我做菜的时候，火那么大，这条头发仍然留了下来。"

Guówáng tīngdào chúshī zhèyàng shuō, yě juéde zhè tiáo tóufa liú zài ròushang hěn yǒu wèntí, jiù wèn: "Yǒurén pèng guo nǐ zuò de cài ma?"
国王听到厨师这样说，也觉得这条头发留在肉上很有问题，就问："有人碰过你做的菜吗？"

Chúshī shuō chu le yī gè rén de míngzi. Jīngguò diàochá hòu, nàge rén chéngrèn le tóufa shì tā gùyì fàng shangqu de.
厨师说出了一个人的名字。经过调查后，那个人承认了头发是他故意放上去的。

Zài guówáng shēngqì
在国王生气

The roasted lamb meat

de shíhou chúshī méiyǒu jǐnzhāng érshì xiǎng le yī gè
的 时候，厨师 没有 紧张，而是 想 了 一 个

hǎo de bànfǎ qù shuōmíng zìjǐ bìng méiyǒu zuò cuò Zhèyàng
好 的 办法 去 说明 自己 并 没有 做 错。这样

bǐ kū zhe qiú guówáng gèng yǒuxiào
比 哭 着 求 国王 更 有效。

❷ Yī tiáo tuǐ de yāzi
一 条 腿 的 鸭子

Yǒu yī gè shāngrén qǐng le yī gè chúshī tā zuò
有 一 个 商人，请 了 一 个 厨师，他 做

de yāzi hěn hǎochī
的 鸭子 很 好吃。

Shāngrén hěn xǐhuan chī chúshī zuò de yāzi dàn
商人 很 喜欢 吃 厨师 做 的 鸭子，但

cónglái méiyǒu gōngkāi shuō guo tā zuò de hǎo
从来 没有 公开 说 过 他 做 得 好。

Yǒu yī cì shāngrén qǐng kèrén chīfàn tèbié gàosu
有 一 次，商人 请 客人 吃饭，特别 告诉

chúshī yào zuò yāzi Dāng yāzi sòng shanglai de shíhou
厨师 要 做 鸭子。当 鸭子 送 上来 的 时候，

shāngrén fāxiàn yāzi zhǐyǒu yī tiáo tuǐ
商人 发现 鸭子 只有 一 条 腿。

Fànhòu shāngrén
饭后，商人

wèn chúshī fāshēng le
问 厨师 发生 了

shénme shì
什么 事。

Chúshī dài shāngrén
厨师 带 商人

láidào chúfáng zhǐ
来到 厨房，指

Peking Duck, China's most famous dish

zhe nàxiē zhèngzài shuìjiào de yāzi shuō Nǐ kàn zhèxiē
着那些正在睡觉的鸭子说：“你看，这些
yāzi dōu shì yī tiáo tuǐ de
鸭子都是一条腿的。”

Shāngrén zhīdao yāzi shuì zháo de shíhou huì bǎ tuǐ
商人知道鸭子睡着的时候，会把腿
shōu qilai jiù xiàng zhǐyǒu yī tiáo tuǐ
收起来，就像只有一条腿。

Tā pāi yi pāi shǒu yào suǒyǒu yāzi dōu zhàn qilai
他拍一拍手，要所有鸭子都站起来。

Shāngrén shuō Xiànzài de yāzi bù shì yǒu liǎng tiáo
商人说：“现在的鸭子不是有两条
tuǐ ma
腿吗？”

Chúshī shuō Duì a Zhǐyǒu nǐ pāishǒu le yāzi
厨师说：“对啊。只有你拍手了，鸭子
cái yǒu liǎng tiáo tuǐ ne
才有两条腿呢！”

Tīngdào zhèlǐ shāngrén zhōngyú míngbai wèntí chū zài
听到这里，商人终于明白问题出在
nǎli le Chúshī zuò le hǎochī de yāzi xūyào biéren
哪里了：厨师做了好吃的鸭子，需要别人
pāi shǒu jiào hǎo ne
拍手叫好呢！

Dāng rénmen nǔlì bǎ shìqing zuòhǎo wǒmen yīnggāi
当人们努力把事情做好，我们应该
biǎoshì gǎnxiè Zhǐyǒu zhèyàng rénmen cái huì bǎ shìqing zuò
表示感谢。只有这样，人们才会把事情做
de gèng hǎo
得更好。

Translation

❶ The hair on the meat

A long time ago, there was an emperor who loved to eat meat.

One day, the emperor was eating his meat when he found a strand of hair on it. He was furious. He summoned the chef and asked him for an explanation.

The chef quickly admitted his mistake, and said there were three things he had done wrong.

The emperor was puzzled, and asked: "What were the three things you did wrong?"

The chef said: "First, my knife did not cut this strand of hair; second, I had cleaned the meat and put it in the pot without discovering this strand of hair; third, the fire was very hot when I was cooking, but this strand of hair still remained on the meat."

Upon hearing what the chef said, the emperor felt there was something amiss with the hair remaining on the meat, and asked him: "Did anyone touch the dish you prepared?"

The chef gave the name of a person. After some investigation, that person admitted he was the one who deliberately put the hair on the meat.

When the emperor was angry, the chef did not panic, but thought of a clever way to say that he did not do any wrong. This was more effective than crying and pleading with the emperor.

❷ A one-legged duck

A businessman hired a chef who cooked excellent ducks.

The businessman liked eating the ducks that the chef prepared, but he had never praised the chef in front of others.

On one occasion, the businessman invited some guests over for a meal, and he specially asked the chef to prepare some ducks. When the ducks were served, the businessman found that all the ducks had only one leg each.

After the meal, the businessman asked the chef what happened.

The chef brought the businessman to the kitchen and pointed to the sleeping ducks: "See, these ducks all have only one leg."

The businessman knew that when ducks sleep, they tuck their legs in, and so they look like they have only one leg.

He clapped his hands to get all the ducks to stand up.

The businessman said: "Don't the ducks have two legs now?"

The chef said: "That's right. The ducks have two legs now that you clapped your hands!"

On hearing this, the businessman finally realized the problem: The chef prepared delicious ducks, and he needed some applause as encouragement!

When people have put in effort to do something well, we should show our appreciation. Only then will they do their jobs even better.

Expansion Reading

Wisdom in food

Chinese people often say: "those living on a mountain live off the mountain; those living near water live off the water." Indeed, the eight major regional cuisines of China reflect the combination of climate, food products, natural environment and other factors that are unique to each region.

The cuisine from southwestern China is known throughout the country. It is unique in its skillful use of various seasonings in preparing food, in particular those that create a hot and spicy taste. People say that is because the southwest region is humid, and eating spicy food can repel the chill and dampness.

In the coastal areas of southeastern China, due to proximity to the sea and dense network of rivers, the cuisine features many ingredients that are taken from the rivers and the sea, and is mainly light and delicate in flavor. Moreover, these areas are hot and humid, and food with a light flavour is good for the body.

In northern China, wheat-based food is extremely popular. In some cities, one can find more than a hundred kinds of wheat-based food in any restaurant on the street. Because northern China produces plenty of the grain, wheat flour has become a staple food. In addition, wheat products have a high energy content, and can help people to keep the cold at bay, as well as boost their energy to give them the strength they need for work.

The cuisines from China are known the world over. When you come to know the interesting stories behind these cuisines, won't you appreciate even more the wisdom that lies in what the Chinese eat?

GAMES FOR FUN

These dishes reflect the unique characteristics of a few regions in China. Can you guess what these regions are?

(1)

(2)

(3)

A. Northern China

B. Southeastern China

C. Southwestern China

Answer: 1—C, 2—A, 3—B

Shàonián yě yǒu dà zhìhuì
少年也有大智慧
Young in age, big on wisdom

Pre-reading Questions

1. There is a Chinese proverb that goes: "Better to despise a poor old man than a poor young man." Do you agree with this saying?
2. Name an example of a young genius from the Western world.

Tiàowǔ de jī
❶ 跳舞 的 鸡

A beautiful red cock

Cáo Chōng shì Cáo Cāo de érzi
曹冲是曹操的儿子。

Yǒu yī cì, yǒurén sòng le yī zhī jī gěi Cáo Cāo. Zhè zhī jī zhǎng de hěn gāo, yǔmáo de yánsè hěn piàoliang. Cáo Cāo fēicháng xǐhuan tā.
有一次，有人送了一只鸡给曹操。这只鸡长得很高，羽毛的颜色很漂亮。曹操非常喜欢它。

Bù zhīdao shénme yuányīn, zhè zhī jī zǒngshì bù
不知道什么原因，这只鸡总是不

chī dōngxi yě bù hēshuǐ kànshangqu hěn méi jīngshen de
吃 东西，也 不 喝水，看上去 很 没 精神 的
yàngzi
样子。

Cáo Cāo wèn shēnbiān de rén Nǐmen nǎge rén néng
曹 操 问 身边 的 人：“你们 哪个 人 能
ràng zhè zhī jī tiàowǔ wǒ jiù gěi tā yī fèn lǐwù
让 这 只 鸡 跳舞，我 就 给 他 一 份 礼物！”

Tīngdào yǒu lǐwù dàjiā dōu xiǎng shì yīxià
听到 有 礼物，大家 都 想 试 一下。
Kěshì tāmen yòng le hěn duō bànfǎ dōu bù néng ràng jī
可是，他们 用 了 很 多 办法，都 不 能 让 鸡
gāoxìng qilai háishi nàge méi jīngshen de yàngzi
高兴 起来，还是 那个 没 精神 的 样子。

Zhèshíhou zhǐyǒu shí duō suì de Cáo Chōng shuō Wǒ
这时候，只有 十 多 岁 的 曹 冲 说：“我
yǒu bànfǎ
有 办法！”

Yuánlái tā de bànfǎ shì ràng rén bǎ yīmiàn dà
原来，他 的 办法 是 让 人 把 一面 大
jìngzi fàng zài jī de miànqián
镜子 放 在 鸡 的 面前。

Shuōlai yě qíguài dāng nà zhī jī kàndào jìngzi lǐmiàn
说来 也 奇怪，当 那 只 鸡 看到 镜子 里面
chūxiàn le yī zhī zhǎng zhe piàoliang yǔmáo de jī shí jiù
出现 了 一 只 长 着 漂亮 羽毛 的 鸡 时，就
mǎshàng jīngshen qilai hěn kāixīn de tiàowǔ
马上 精神 起来，很 开心 地 跳舞。

Cáo Cāo kàndào jī guǒrán tiàowǔ le jiù sònggěi tā
曹 操 看到 鸡 果然 跳舞 了，就 送给 他
yī fèn xiǎo lǐwù
一 份 小 礼物。

Shù zài kǒu zhōng

❷ 树在口中

Yǒu yī gè xiǎo háizi jīngcháng dào fùjìn yī gè lǎorén
有一个小孩子经常到附近一个老人
de jiāli wán Yīnwèi lǎorén de yuànzi hěn dà hòubian
的家里玩。因为老人的院子很大，后边
hái zhòng yǒu yī kē hěn gāo de shù
还种有一棵很高的树。

Yǒu yī tiān tā láidào lǎorén de jiā kàndào lǎorén
有一天，他来到老人的家，看到老人
zhèngzài ràng rén bǎ nà kē dà shù nòng zǒu
正在让人把那棵大树弄走。

Xiǎohái juéde qíguài jiù wèn lǎorén Nǐ wèishénme
小孩觉得奇怪，就问老人：“你为什么
nòng zǒu zhè kē shù ne Tā bìng le ma
弄走这棵树呢？它病了吗？”

Lǎorén shuō Tā méi bìng Wǒ zhè yuànzi sìsìfāngfāng
老人说：“它没病。我这院子四四方方
de zhōngjiān zhǎng zhe zhème yī kē shù kànshangqu hǎoxiàng
的，中间长着这么一棵树，看上去好像
yī gè kùn zì Wǒ bèi kùn zhu le yǐhòu zuò shì kěndìng
一个‘困’字。我被困住了，以后做事肯定
bù shùnlì Suǒyǐ wǒ juédìng bù yào zhè kē shù le
不顺利。所以，我决定不要这棵树了。”

Tīng le lǎorén de huà xiǎohái xiào zhe shuō Zhào nǐ
听了老人的话，小孩笑着说：“照你
de yìsi rúguǒ nǐ bǎ zhè kē shù nòng zǒu zhè yuànzi jiù
的意思，如果你把这棵树弄走，这院子就
zhǐyǒu nǐ yī gè rén le nà bù yòu chéng le yī gè qiú
只有你一个人了，哪不又成了一个‘囚’
zì Nǐ bèi guān qilai le yǐhòu hái néng zuòshì ma
字？你被关起来了，以后还能做事吗？”

Lǎorén tīng le xiǎohái de huà, juéde tā shuō de yǒu
老人听了小孩的话，觉得他说得有

dàoli, jiù liúxia nà kē shù le.
道理，就留下那棵树了。

Translation

❶ The dancing chicken

Cao Chong was the son of Cao Cao.

Someone once sent Cao Cao a chicken. This chicken was tall, and the colour of its feathers were beautiful. Cao Cao liked it very much.

For some unknown reason, this chicken did not eat or drink anything, and it was extremely listless.

Cao Cao told the people around him: "If anyone of you can make this chicken dance, I will give him a gift!"

Upon hearing there would be a reward, everyone wanted to give it a try. But no matter what they did, they could not make the chicken happy, and it still looked listless.

At that moment, Cao Chong, who was only ten years old, said: "I have an idea!"

It turned out that his idea was to place a large mirror in front of the chicken.

Strange as it may sound, when the chicken saw in the mirror another chicken with beautiful feathers, it immediately became lively and danced happily.

Cao Cao saw that the chicken was indeed dancing, and so he gave his son a small gift.

❷ A tree in a square

There was a child who often played at the house of an old man who lived nearby. Behind the house was a large square courtyard, and in the middle was a tall tree.

One day, the child came to the old man's house, and saw that the old man was trying to get rid of the tree.

The child was puzzled, and so he asked the old man: "Why are you getting rid of this tree? Is it sick?"

The old man said: "No, it's not sick. I have a tree growing in the middle of my square courtyard, and this resembles the character kun. Things will not go well when I am stuck by this tree, and so it has to go."

Upon hearing this, the child smiled and said: "Based on what you said, if you remove the tree, there would be just ren left. Won't that look like the character qiu? Will you be able do anything when you are locked up?"

The old man thought the child's words made sense, and so he kept the tree.

Expansion Reading

Outstanding youths

There is an old saying in China called *yingxiong chu shaonian*（英雄出少年）, which means heroic figures start to achieve a lot from a young age.

A long time ago, there was a youth called Gan Luo. He bravely went to his king to recommend himself as an envoy leading a diplomatic mission to another state. Using his wits, he convinced the other state to voluntarily cede five cities to his king, and war was avoided as a result. Gan did very well in his mission, and he even returned with plenty of treasure. The king was delighted, and made an exception to appoint him as a key official to manage state affairs. At that time, Gan was only twelve years old.

Yue Yun was also an outstanding youth. His father was a famous general in ancient China. On one occasion, some enemies attacked Yue's home when his father happened to be away. Yue led the youths in his household to fight the attackers. The enemies saw that Yue was just a boy, and did not think much of him. Unknown to them, Yue had been trained in literary and martial arts from a tender age, and was brave and resourceful. He led his family to defeat the enemy. Yue later joined his father's army, where he won several victories on the battlefield and attained countless achievements.

The wisdom of youth need not be inferior to that of adults. We should not belittle those who are young.

GAMES FOR FUN

Looking at the scenario shown below, how would you save the child inside the water vat?

Answer

In ancient China, there was a brilliant child who encountered a similar situation. His solution was to smash the vat to rescue the child who had fallen inside. Can you think of more solutions?

Zěnyàng guǎnlǐ hǎo guójiā

怎样管理好国家

How to govern a nation

Pre-reading Questions

1. There is a Chinese idiom that goes: "A conceited army is bound to be defeated" Do you agree with this saying?
2. The Chinese people believe that "one can infer the whole by observing a small part." Can you name an example?

Jiéyuē de guówáng

❶ 节约 的 国王

Sòngtàizǔ shì Zhōngguó qízhōng
宋太祖 是 中国 其中
yī gè hǎo guówáng. Tā yǐqián
一 个 好 国王。他 以前
shì jūnrén, suīrán zuò le
是 军人，虽然 做 了
guówáng, rìcháng de shēnghuó
国王，日常 的 生活
réngrán hěn jiéyuē. Tā rènwéi
仍然 很 节约。他 认为
yào guǎnlǐ hǎo guójiā, shǒuxiān
要 管理 好 国家，首先

Emperor Song Taizu

yào guǎnlǐ hǎo zìjǐ
要管理好自己。

Yǒu yī cì tā kàndào yī zhī yǐqián guówáng yòng guo de bēizi hěn shēngqì
有一次，他看到一只以前国王用过的杯子，很生气。

Tā duì shēnbiān de guānyuán shuō Zhège zhǐshì tā wǎnshang yòng de bēizi shàngmian dōu yǒu zhème duō bǎoshí Nàme tā chīfàn yòng de dōngxi bù shì gèngjiā huāqián ma Yǒu zhèyàng de guówáng rénmen zěnme huì shēnghuó de hǎo ne
他对身边的官员说："这个只是他晚上用的杯子，上面都有这么多宝石。那么他吃饭用的东西，不是更加花钱吗？有这样的国王，人们怎么会生活得好呢？"

Yòu yǒu yī cì Sòngtàizǔ de jiějie lái kàn tā Tā shēnshang chuān le yī jiàn yòng niǎo máo zhìzào de yīfu shífēn piàoliang
又有一次，宋太祖的姐姐来看他。她身上穿了一件用鸟毛制造的衣服，十分漂亮。

Sòngtàizǔ kàndào zhè jiàn yīfu hěn bù gāoxìng de shuō Nǐ yǐhòu bù yào chuān zhè jiàn yīfu le
宋太祖看到这件衣服，很不高兴地说："你以后不要穿这件衣服了。"

Jiějie shuō Wèishénme ne Yīfushang de niǎo máo yòng bù le duōshǎo qián
姐姐说："为什么呢？衣服上的鸟毛用不了多少钱。"

Sòngtàizǔ shuō Zhè bù shì yī jiàn xiǎoshì a
宋太祖说："这不是一件小事啊！

An exquisite teacup

Nǐ chuān shàng zhè jiàn
你穿上这件

yīfu biéren juéde
衣服，别人觉得

hǎokàn jiù huì xuéxí
好看，就会学习

nǐ yòng niǎo máo lái
你，用鸟毛来

zuò yīfu Dàjiā
做衣服。大家

dōu qù zhuā zhè zhǒng niǎo tāmen hěn kuài jiù bèi zhuā guāng
都去抓这种鸟，它们很快就被抓光。

Rénmen yǐhòu zài yě kàn bù dào zhè zhǒng niǎo le
人们以后再也看不到这种鸟了。”

Jiějie tīng le guówáng de huà juéde tā shuō de hěn
姐姐听了国王的话，觉得他说得很

yǒu dàoli jiù bǎ yīfu tuō xialai yǐhòu bùzài chuān
有道理，就把衣服脱下来，以后不再穿

le
了。

Táozi hé jiāngjūn
❷ 桃子和将军

Cóngqián yǒu sān gè hěn yǒu nénglì de jiāngjūn wèi
从前，有三个很有能力的将军，为

guójiā qǔdé duō cì zhàndòu de shènglì
国家取得多次战斗的胜利。

Hòulái tāmen dōu juéde guójiā bù néng méiyǒu
后来，他们都觉得国家不能没有

tāmen Tāmen kànbuqǐ qítā guānyuán duì guówáng yě
他们。他们看不起其它官员，对国王也

yuèláiyuè bù lǐmào
越来越不礼貌。

Guówáng hé shēnbiān de guānyuán duì tāmen hěn bù
国王 和 身边 的 官员 对 他们 很 不
fàngxīn hàipà tāmen jiānglái huì wēihài guójiā
放心，害怕 他们 将来 会 危害 国家。

Yǒu yī cì guówáng qǐng sān gè jiāngjūn hé qítā
有 一 次，国王 请 三 个 将军 和 其它
guānyuán chīfàn Fànhòu guówáng qǐng dàjiā chī wàidì sòng
官员 吃饭。饭后，国王 请 大家 吃 外地 送
lai de táozi Zuìhòu zhǐyǒu liǎng gè táozi méi chī
来 的 桃子。最后，只有 两 个 桃子 没 吃。

Yī gè guānyuán jiànyì guówáng bǎ zhè liǎng gè táozi
一 个 官员 建议 国王 把 这 两 个 桃子
sònggěi zuì yǒu nénglì de jiāngjūn
送给 最 有 能力 的 将军。

Zhè sān gè jiāngjūn dōu rènwéi zìjǐ zuì yǒu nénglì
这 三 个 将军 都 认为 自己 最 有 能力，
bù bǎ lìngwài liǎng rén fàng zài yǎn nèi Suīrán juéde zhège
不 把 另外 两 人 放 在 眼 内。虽然 觉得 这个
jiànyì yǒu wèntí wèile chī dào táozi tāmen sān rén
建议 有 问题，为了 吃 到 桃子，他们 三 人
zài guówáng miànqián háishi dǎ qilai
在 国王 面前 还是 打 起来。

Yóuyú sān gè jiāngjūn de shílì hěn jiējìn jiéguǒ liǎng
由于 三 个 将军 的 实力 很 接近，结果 两
gè sǐ le yī gè shòu
个 死 了，一 个 受
le hěn zhòng de shāng
了 很 重 的 伤。
Zhèshíhou shòushāng de
这时候，受伤 的
jiāngjūn zhōngyú míngbai zhè
将军 终于 明白 这

Peaches

shì guówáng ānpái de jìhuà. Tā zhīdao táo bù diào jiù
是 国王 安排 的 计划。他 知道 逃 不 掉，就
zài guówáng miànqián zìshā le
在 国王 面前 自杀 了。

Dāng yī gè rén tài guò xiāngxìn zìjǐ de nénglì shì
当 一 个 人 太 过 相信 自己 的 能力，是
zuì róngyì fàncuò de
最 容易 犯错 的。

Translation

❶ The frugal emperor

Song Taizu was one of the great emperors of China. A former soldier who became emperor, he remained frugal in his everyday life. He believed that in order to govern a nation well, he must first manage himself properly.

On one occasion, he saw a cup used by the previous emperor, and he became very angry.

He said to an official beside him: “This is only a cup that he used in the evenings, yet there are so many precious stones on it. Then what about the tableware he used for his meals? Wouldn’t they cost even more? With a ruler like that, how can the people live a good life?”

On another occasion, Song Taizu’s elder sister came to visit him. She was wearing a beautiful garment that was made from bird feathers.

When Song Taizu saw the garment, he said with displeasure: “Do not wear this garment again.”

His sister asked: “Why? The feathers on this garment cost quite a lot of money.”

Song Taizu replied: “This is no small matter! If you wear this garment, and other people think it looks nice, they will learn from you and make clothes from bird feathers. If everyone were to go catch this breed of bird, they will soon be all captured. People will not be able to see this bird again."

When the sister heard what the emperor said, she thought his words made sense. She took the garment off and never wore it again.

❷ Peaches and generals

There were three capable generals who had won many battles for their country.

Eventually they felt that the country could not do without them. They looked down on other officials, and became increasingly disrespectful to the emperor.

The emperor and his officials were wary of these generals, as they were worried that they might pose a threat to the country in future.

On one occasion, the emperor invited the three generals and other officials to a meal. After the meal, the emperor invited everyone to eat peaches that were brought in from elsewhere. In the end, only two peaches were left.

An official suggested that the emperor give these two peaches to the most capable general.

The three generals each thought they were the most capable, and did not regard the other two as a worthy match. Although they felt that something was not quite right with this suggestion, they started fighting for the peaches in front of the emperor.

As the three generals were closely matched, in the end two died and one was seriously injured. The injured general finally realized this was a ploy arranged by the emperor. He knew he could not escape, and so he killed himself in front of the emperor.

When a person is too confident of his own ability, he is most vulnerable to making mistakes.

Expansion Reading

Wise emperors

Throughout the ages, during various dynasties in China, there were many wise emperors. They not only governed the country well, but were also adept in managing diplomatic relations with other countries.

The Tang Dynasty was a powerful period in the history of China. The prosperity of the Tang Dynasty started with the reign of Tang Taizong. After Tang Taizong became the emperor, he did not indulge in a life of pleasure, but instead he became increasingly diligent. He appointed exemplary talents as officials, accepted beneficial proposals from his ministers, and even reduced taxes on his people. He implemented a series of policies that gradually led to an orderly society, as well as a peaceful and prosperous life for his people. In foreign affairs, he expanded China's borders, and implemented enlightened policies to treat ethnic minorities well and gain their support. These measures made China the world's most powerful empire at the time.

There were also Emperor Wudi of the Han Dynasty, Emperor Hongwu of the Ming Dynasty and Emperor Qianlong of the Qing Dynasty. During their reign over China, all these emperors expanded China's territory and increased its production capabilities. With their efforts, China became powerful and prosperous. China became one of the world's leading countries at the time, and had a significant influence on the rest of the world.

Hǎo de guǎnlǐ

好的管理

An enlightened governance

Pre-reading Questions

1. If someone around you is troubled by some minor matters, how would you cheer him or her up?
2. If you have discovered a talented person, and you would like him to work for you, what would you do to persuade him?

Guówáng de wǎnhuì

❶ 国王 的 晚会

Cóngqián yī gè guówáng jǔbàn le yī gè wǎnhuì

从前，一 个 国王 举办 了 一 个 晚会。

Guówáng de fūrén men

国王 的 夫人 们

dōu cānjiā le

都 参加 了。

Zài wǎnhuìshang

在 晚会上，

dàjiā yīqǐ hējiǔ

大家 一起 喝酒，

fēicháng gāoxìng

非常 高兴。

The Manchurian king and queen of the Qing Dynasty

Tūrán dà fēng chuī guò bǎ dēnghuǒ miè le
突然，大风吹过，把灯火灭了。
Zhèshíhou yǒu gè guānyuán cuòwù de lāzhu le yī gè
这时候，有个官员错误地拉住了一个
fūrén de shǒu Dāng tā bìkāi shí bǎ zhège guānyuán
夫人的手。当她避开时，把这个官员
yīfushang de dàizi lā duàn le
衣服上的带子拉断了。

Fūrén huídào guówáng de shēnbiān qǐngqiú guówáng bǎ
夫人回到国王的身边，请求国王把
nàge guānyuán zhǎo chulai
那个官员找出来。

Guówáng duì shēnbiān de guānyuán shuō Bùyòng zài diǎndēng
国王对身边的官员说：“不用再点灯
le jiù zhèyàng tīng yīnyuè ba
了，就这样听音乐吧。”

Fūrén tīng le guówáng de huà hěn bù gāoxìng
夫人听了国王的话，很不高兴。

Guówáng duì tā shuō Zhè cì wǎnhuì shì wèile ràng
国王对她说：“这次晚会，是为了让
wǒmen gēn guānyuán men de guānxì gèng hǎo yīdiǎn Méiyǒu
我们跟官员们的关系更好一点。没有
dēng de shíhou bù xiǎoxīn lāzhu nǐ de shǒu bìng bù shì
灯的时候，不小心拉住你的手，并不是
shénme dà de cuò Rúguǒ wǒ bǎ tā zhǎo chulai zhǐ huì
什么大的错。如果我把他找出来，只会
ràng dàjiā dōu bù gāoxìng le
让大家都不高兴了。”

Jǐ nián hòu guówáng dàilǐng jūnduì gēn biéguó de jūnduì
几年后，国王带领军队跟别国的军队
zuòzhàn Yī gè jiāngjūn yǒnggǎn de zhàndòu qǔdé le hěn
作战。一个将军勇敢地战斗，取得了很

duō cì shènglì Tā jiùshì wǎnhuìshang fàn le xiǎo cuò de
多次胜利。他就是晚会上犯了小错的
rén
人。

Yuánlái dāng biéren fàn le xiǎo cuò de shíhou zhuāzhu
原来，当别人犯了小错的时候，抓住
bù fàng bù yīdìng shì duì de
不放不一定是对的。

❷ Sǐ mǎ huàn hǎo mǎ
死马换好马

Èrqiān duō nián qián Zhōngguó de tǔdìshang yǒu hěn duō
二千多年前，中国的土地上有很多
xiǎo guójiā
小国家。

Qízhōng yī gè xiǎo guó de guówáng hěn xiǎng zhǎo yǒu
其中一个小国的国王，很想找有
běnshi de rén lái bāngzhù tā shǐ guójiā qiángdà qilai
本事的人来帮助他，使国家强大起来。
Kěshì rénmen dōu bù xiāngxìn tā méiyǒu rén yuànyì tì
可是，人们都不相信他，没有人愿意替
tā zuòshì
他做事。

Zhǎo bù dào yǒu běnshi de rén zhège guówáng hěn bù
找不到有本事的人，这个国王很不
kāixīn
开心。

Yǒu yī tiān yī gè lǎorén láidào guówáng miànqián gěi
有一天，一个老人来到国王面前，给
tā jiǎng le yī gè gùshi
他讲了一个故事：

Yǒu yī gè guówáng yuànyì huā hěn duō hěn duō
"有一个国王愿意花很多很多

Bronze chariot

qián qù mǎi yī zhī
钱去买一只
hǎo mǎ kěshì tā
好马，可是他
yīzhí méiyǒu mǎi dào
一直没有买到。
Hòulái tā zhīdao
后来，他知道
yǒu gè dìfang yǒu
有个地方有
hǎo mǎ jiù pài rén qù mǎi Kěshì mǎi huilai de zhǐshì
好马，就派人去买。可是买回来的，只是
yī zhī sǐ mǎ hái huā le hěn duō qián
一只死马，还花了很多钱。”

Mǎi mǎ de rén duì guówáng shuō Dàjiā kàndào
“买马的人对国王说：‘大家看到
nǐ huā zhème duō qián mǎi yī zhī sǐ le de mǎ jiù huì
你花这么多钱买一只死了的马，就会
xiāngxìn guówáng zhēnde xiǎng dédào hǎo mǎ zìrán yǒurén
相信国王真的想得到好马，自然有人
yuànyì bǎ huó de hǎo mǎ mài gěi nǐ
愿意把活的好马卖给你。’”

Hòulái zhège guówáng zhēnde mǎi dào le sān zhī hǎo
“后来，这个国王真的买到了三只好
mǎ
马。”

Wǒ rènwéi xiàng wǒ zhèzhǒng nénglì píngcháng de rén
“我认为，像我这种能力平常的人
dōu nénggòu dédào nǐ de zhòngshì nàxiē yǒu běnshi de rén
都能够得到你的重视，那些有本事的人
yīdìng huì míngbai nǐ de xiǎngfǎ
一定会明白你的想法。”

Guówáng tīng wán zhège rén de huà míngbai dào yào
国王听完这个人的话，明白到要
biéren zhīchí zìjǐ jiùyào zhǔdòng biǎomíng zìjǐ de
别人支持自己，就要主动表明自己的
tàidu Yúshì tā gěi zhège lǎorén ānpái le yī gè
态度。于是，他给这个老人安排了一个
hěn zhòngyào de zhíwèi
很重要的职位。

Guò le bùjiǔ hěn duō yǒu běnshi de rén dōu zhǔdòng
过了不久，很多有本事的人都主动
lái zhǎo guówáng le Shíjǐ nián hòu zhège xiǎo guó chéngwéi
来找国王了。十几年后，这个小国成为
le dāngshí zuì qiángdà de guójiā
了当时最强大的国家。

Translation

❶ The king's evening party

A long time ago, a king held an evening party. The king's concubines also attended the party.

During the party, everyone was drinking wine and having a good time.

Suddenly, a gust of wind blew the lights out of the lamps. At that moment, one of the officials mistakenly grabbed the hand of one of the king's concubines. While she was pulling herself away, she broke a belt on the official's clothes.

The king's concubine returned to the side of the king. She asked the king to find out who the offending official was.

The king said to another official beside him: "There's no need to light the lamps again. Let's listen to the music like this."

When the concubine heard what the king said, she was not happy.

The king said to her: "This party was held to improve relationships with our officials. While the lights were out, someone grabbed your hand by accident, but that was not a big mistake. If I were to identify who that official was, it will only make everyone unhappy."

A few years later, the king led his army to fight the army of another country. One of his generals fought valiantly and achieved several victories. He was the official who had made that minor mistake during the party.

So, when other people have made a minor mistake, punishing them may not always be the correct thing to do.

❷ Trading a dead horse for a good horse

More than two thousand years ago, there were many small kingdoms in China.

The ruler of one of the small kingdoms wanted to find capable people to assist him in making his kingdom powerful. But no one believed in him, and no one was willing to work for him.

This king was unhappy because he was unable to find any capable people.

One day, an old man came to the king and told him a story:

"A king was willing to spend a lot of money to buy a good horse, but he was unable to buy one. Later, he learnt of a place with good horses, and he sent his men to buy one. But what he got was a dead horse, and it still cost him a lot of money.

"The person who bought the horse told the king: 'When people see that you spent so much money to buy a dead horse, they will believe that you really want to get a good horse, and naturally people will be willing to sell you a good live horse.'

"Later, this king indeed managed to buy three good horses.

"I believe that, if people with average ability like me can gain your recognition, then people with great ability will surely understand what you are thinking."

After the king listened to the old man, he realized that in order for people to support him, he must first make his position clear to others. And so he arranged for this old man to take on an important post.

Soon after, many capable people came to find the king on their own accord. More than a decade later, this small kingdom became one of the most powerful kingdoms at the time.

Expansion Reading

To value talents and use them wisely

Throughout China's history, the progress of a dynasty or an organization has often depended on the leader's ability, especially his ability to manage people. One who can acquire many talents is one who can govern the country well. Outstanding leaders know how to value talent and use it wisely.

Take for example Liu Bang, the founding emperor of the Han Dynasty. He was not particularly outstanding in terms of literary or fighting skills. But he was able to amass many talented people who were adept in warfare and were extremely resourceful, and he assigned them duties in the respective areas in which they excelled. This was how he could overcome stronger rivals and take over the empire.

Emperor Tang Taizong of the Tang Dynasty was also known for his emphasis on choosing and using talent. When he was choosing talented people, he did not care much about their family background. Instead, he placed more importance on their true ability. Wei Zheng was an able assistant who the emperor trusted greatly. Wei was often able to give Tang Taizong the right advice, and pointed out the areas in which the emperor did not do well. In fact, Wei was originally from a

Emperor Tang Taizong

faction that was opposed to Tang Taizong.
Tang Taizong broke the boundary between the aristocracy and the common people. So long as a person was capable, and could suggest excellent proposals, he could be appointed as an official even if he was a commoner. Conversely, if a person was lacking in ability, he would not receive a high post and generous salary even if he was a member of the nobility.
This management philosophy that values talent has remained to this day, and continues to influence generation after generation of Chinese people.

Zuò gè cōngming de rén

做个聪明的人

To be a wise person

Pre-reading Questions

1. Have you ever had the experience of being able to foresee danger? How would you develop such an ability?
2. Have you ever met people who are calculative? How would you get along with them?

Bǎohù zìjǐ

❶ 保护 自己

Ancient Chinese coins

Cóngqián yǒu yī gè jiāngjūn hěn yǒu nénglì, wèi guójiā qǔdé duō cì shènglì. Guówáng hěn zhòngshì tā, duì tā hěn hǎo.

从前，有一个将军很有能力，为国家取得多次胜利。国王很重视他，对他很好。

zhège jiāngjūn wèile zuòhǎo guówáng jiāogěi tā de gōngzuò qǐng le hěn duō yǒu běnshi de rén lái bāngzhù tā

这个将军为了做好国王交给他的工作，请了很多有本事的人来帮助他。

Zhèxiē wèi jiāngjūn gōngzuò de rén dāngzhōng yǒu yī gè
这些为将军工作的人当中，有一个
niánqīngrén Jiāngjūn hěn xǐhuan tā rènwéi tā yīdìng kěyǐ
年轻人。将军很喜欢他，认为他一定可以
zài quánguó kǎoshì zhōng qǔdé dì-yī míng
在全国考试中取得第一名。

Bùguò zhège niánqīngrén tì jiāngjūn gōngzuò de
不过，这个年轻人替将军工作的
shíhou fāxiàn tā píngcháng de shēnghuó hěn làngfèi Tā
时候，发现他平常的生活很浪费。他
bùdàn kànbuqǐ qítā guānyuán érqiě jīngcháng gōngkāi pīpíng
不但看不起其它官员，而且经常公开批评
tāmen Niánqīngrén rènwéi jiāngjūn zhèyàng zuò jiānglái huì chū
他们。年轻人认为将军这样做将来会出
wèntí
问题。

Yǒu yī tiān zhège niánqīngrén duì yī gè hǎo péngyou
有一天，这个年轻人对一个好朋友
shuō Jiāngjūn de hǎo rìzi yīdìng guò bù liǎo duōjiǔ
说："将军的好日子一定过不了多久。
Wǒmen gǎnkuài líkāi ba
我们赶快离开吧。"

Péngyou bù xiāngxìn tā de huà Niánqīngrén wèile bǎohù
朋友不相信他的话。年轻人为了保护
zìjǐ juédìng yī gè rén líkāi
自己，决定一个人离开。

Jiāngjūn méi bànfǎ liúzhu tā zhǐhǎo ràng tā zǒu hái
将军没办法留住他，只好让他走，还
sònggěi tā hěn duō qián
送给他很多钱。

Guò le bùjiǔ guówáng duì jiāngjūn zuò guo de yīxiē
过了不久，国王对将军做过的一些

shìqing hěn bù mǎnyì. Jiāshàng hěn duō guānyuán shuō tā bù
事情很不满意。加上很多官员说他不

hǎo de huà, jiù bǎ tā zhuā le qǐlái, hái bǎ suǒyǒu bāng
好的话，就把他抓了起来，还把所有帮

tā zuòshì de rén yīqǐ zhuā zǒu.
他做事的人一起抓走。

Suīrán niánqīngrén céngjīng wèi jiāngjūn zuòshì, yīnwèi
虽然年轻人曾经为将军做事，因为

líkāi le tā, jiù méiyǒu bèi rén zhuā zǒu. Hòulái tā hái
离开了他，就没有被人抓走。后来他还

zài quánguó kǎoshì zhōng qǔdé dì-yī míng.
在全国考试中取得第一名。

Dǒngde bǎohù zìjǐ, cáishì zhēnzhèng yǒu běnshi de
懂得保护自己，才是真正有本事的

rén.
人。

❷ Jìsuàn 计算

Cóngqián, yǒu yī gè niánqīngrén zhù zài shānshang. Tā
从前，有一个年轻人住在山上。他

měitiān dōu yào dào shānxià de xiǎohé qù dǎ shuǐ.
每天都要到山下的小河去打水。

Yǒu yī tiān, yī gè rén yě xīwàng néng zhù zài
有一天，一个人也希望能住在

shānshang. Tā yīlái, jiù bǎ fángzi li de shuǐ hē guāng le.
山上。他一来，就把房子里的水喝光了。

Niánqīngrén ràng tā qù dǎ shuǐ. Tā jiù yào tóng niánqīngrén gēn
年轻人让他去打水。他就要同年轻人跟

tā yīqǐ qù. Zuìhòu, tāmen yīqǐ bǎ zhuāng mǎn le
他一起去。最后，他们一起把装满了

shuǐ de xiāngzi ná huiqu. Liǎng gè rén juéde zhèyàng cái
水的箱子拿回去。两个人觉得这样才

A pot used for collecting water

gōngpíng shuí yě méiyǒu duō
公平，谁也没有多
zuò yīdiǎn gōngfu
做一点功夫。

Jǐ tiān hòu yòu yǒu yī
几天后，又有一
gè rén yào zhù dào shānshang
个人要住到山上。
Tā yào hēshuǐ niánqīngrén yòu ràng tā zìjǐ qù dǎ shuǐ
他要喝水，年轻人又让他自己去打水。
Tā bǎ shuǐ dǎ huilai zhīhòu jiù zìjǐ yī gè rén hē
他把水打回来之后，就自己一个人喝
guāng le
光了。

Niánqīngrén hé dì-èr gè rén dōu hěn shēngqì tāmen
年轻人和第二个人都很生气，他们
juéde yīnggāi yóu dì-sān gè rén qù dǎ shuǐ Dàn dì-sān gè
觉得应该由第三个人去打水。但第三个
rén juéde bù yīnggāi tā zìjǐ yī gè rén qù Zhèyàng
人觉得不应该他自己一个人去。这样，
shuí dōu bù yuànyì duō chū yīdiǎn lì hěn kuài shānshang
谁都不愿意多出一点力，很快，山上
yīdiǎn shuǐ dōu méiyǒu le sān gè rén dōu méi shuǐ hē
一点水都没有了，三个人都没水喝。

Yī tiān wǎnshang yóudēng bèi nòng dǎo shānshang qǐ le
一天晚上，油灯被弄倒，山上起了
dàhuǒ Sān gè rén zhè cái jí le yīqǐ hézuò bùzài
大火。三个人这才急了，一起合作，不再
jìsuàn shuí yīnggāi zuò duō yīxiē zhōngyú hélì bǎ huǒ miè le
计算谁应该做多一些，终于合力把火灭了。

Hěn duō shíhou wǒmen dōu bù yīnggāi jìsuàn zìjǐ
很多时候，我们都不应该计算自己

dédào duōshǎo shīqù duōshǎo Yīnwèi nǐ shīqù de
得到多少，失去多少。因为，你失去的

yīdiǎndiǎn wǎngwǎng huì dàilai gèng duō de hǎochu
一点点，往往会带来更多的好处。

Translation

❶ Protecting oneself

A long time ago, there was a capable general who helped his country achieve many victories. The emperor thought highly of him and treated him well.

In order to handle the tasks that the emperor had assigned him, this general had many capable people to assist him.

There was a young man among the people who were working for the general. The general liked him, and believed he would surely obtain the top score in the nationwide examinations.

However, this young man found that the general was living a lavish lifestyle. Not only did the general look down on other officials, he often criticized them openly. The young man believed that the general's actions would get him into trouble in future.

In due course, this young man confided in a friend: "The good days of this general are numbered. Let us leave quickly."

His friend did not believe him. In order to protect himself, the young man decided to leave on his own.

The general was unable to persuade him to stay, and so had to let him go. He even gave him a lot of money.

Soon after, the emperor was not pleased with some of the things that the general had done, and many officials were complaining about him. And so the emperor had the general captured along with those who had worked for him.

Although the young man used to work for the general, he was not captured as he had already left him. The young man later obtained the top score in the nationwide examinations.

A truly capable person is one who knows to protect himself.

❷ To be calculating

A long time ago, there was a young man who lived on a mountain. Every day he would go down the mountain to collect water from a stream.

One day, another man also wanted to live on the mountain. When he came, he drank all the water in the house. The young man asked him to go collect water. The other man insisted that the young man go with him. In the end, they filled a tank with water and brought it back. Both men felt that this was fair, as no one had to put in more effort than the other person.

A few days later, another man wanted to live on the mountain. He too wanted to drink water, and so the young man asked him to go collect his own water f. After he came back with the water, he drank it all by himself.

The young man and the second man were angry. They felt that the third man should collect water for all of them. And so, none of them wanted to put in more effort than the rest. Soon there was not a drop of water left on the mountain, and none of the three men had water to drink.

One night, an oil lamp got knocked over, and there was a big fire on the mountain. Only then did the three men panic. They worked together, and were not concerned about who was putting in more effort, and finally put the fire out together.

Many times, we should not be too calculating about how much we have gained or lost. This is because a little something lost can often bring us even more benefit.

The Chinese who know how to protect themselves

Protecting oneself and concealing one's strengths are two rules of conduct that are advocated in traditional Chinese thinking.

People have been taught from a young age that when they encounter an unexpected situation, they should consider the actual circumstances and protect themselves first before doing anything else. If the situation is adverse, one should leave without delay. Today, many people are opposed to such a practice. They feel this could make people irresponsible, and not intervene even when they see something wrong. But there are others who feel differently: If a person cannot even protect himself, how can he possibly do anything worthwhile?

In their work and social life, people tend to think they should conceal their strengths, and reveal them only when the need arises. There is a saying in China called *shudazhaofeng*（树大招风）, which means a person who flaunts his abilities will attract the envy of others, and along with it a lot of unnecessary trouble. That is why when people praise a Chinese person, he will usually deny it. To the Chinese people, this is not hypocrisy, but a display of modesty, and is considered a virtue.

Of course, protecting oneself and concealing one's strengths should be applied within reasonable limits. If a person is overly concerned with protecting himself or concealing his ability, and does not react or perform when he should, the Chinese also consider this as inappropriate behavior.

Jiàoyù de fāngfǎ

教育的方法

Tips on teaching

Pre-reading Questions

1. If you are a supervisor, and your subordinates do not accept your authority, what would you do to resolve this problem?
2. What do you think is the most important principle in educating children?

Sūn Wǔ xùnliàn jūnrén

❶ 孙武训练军人

Sūn Wǔ shì Zhōngguó gǔdài yī gè hěn yǒu nénglì de jūnshìjiā

孙武是中国古代一个很有能力的军事家。

Yǒu yī cì tā gēn guówáng shuōqi xùnliàn jūnrén de shìqing Guówáng xiǎng kǎoyàn tā de lǐngdǎo nénglì yào tā xùnliàn yī duì nǚ jūnrén

有一次，他跟国王说起训练军人的事情。国王想考验他的领导能力，要他训练一队女军人。

Sūn Wǔ xuǎn chu le yībǎi gè pǔtōng de nǚhái hái

孙武选出了一百个普通的女孩，还

ràng guówáng de liǎng gè fūrén
让国王的两个夫人
dāng le duìzhǎng
当了队长。

Xùnliàn kāishǐ de shíhou
训练开始的时候，
Sūn Wǔ gàosu zhèxiē nǚhái
孙武告诉这些女孩：
Xiànzài nǐmen shì jūnrén
“现在你们是军人，
bìxū ànzhào mìnglìng qù zuò
必须按照命令去做。
Bù jiēshòu mìnglìng de rén huì
不接受命令的人，会
shòudào chǔfèn
受到处分。”

The Warrior Statues

Kěshì Sūn Wǔ shuō chu le mìnglìng méiyǒu yī gè
可是，孙武说出了命令，没有一个
nǚhái ànzhào tā de huà zuò
女孩按照他的话做。

Sūn Wǔ bǎ mìnglìng chóngfù shuō yī cì hái yāoqiú liǎng
孙武把命令重复说一次，还要求两
gè duìzhǎng shǒuxiān zuòhǎo Bùguò nà liǎng gè fūrén zhǐshì
个队长首先做好。不过，那两个夫人只是
zhàn zài yībiān shuōshuoxiàoxiao jiù xiàng méi tīngdào tā de
站在一边说说笑笑，就像没听到他的
shuōhuà
说话。

Sūn Wǔ duì zhèxiē nǚhái shuō Liǎng gè duìzhǎng suīrán
孙武对这些女孩说：“两个队长虽然
shì guówáng de fūrén tāmen bù jiēshòu mìnglìng bìxū
是国王的夫人，她们不接受命令，必须

shòudào chǔfèn
受到 处分。”

Shuō wán zhè jù huà, Sūn Wǔ jiù jiào rén bǎ liǎng gè fūrén shā le.
说 完 这 句 话，孙 武 就 叫 人 把 两 个 夫人 杀 了。

Zhèxiē nǚhái hěn hàipà, mǎshàng ànzhào Sūn Wǔ de mìnglìng rènzhēn de xùnliàn. Jǐ gè yuè zhīhòu, zhèxiē nǚhái dōu chéngwéi le zhēnzhèng de jūnrén.
这些 女孩 很 害怕，马上 按照 孙 武 的 命令 认真 地 训练。几 个 月 之后，这些 女孩 都 成为 了 真正 的 军人。

Tīngshuō Sūn Wǔ zài xùnliàn de shíhou bù zěn shuōhuà, dàn tā shuō guo de huà, jiù yīdìng yào zuòdào.
听说 孙 武 在 训练 的 时候 不 怎 说话，但 他 说 过 的 话，就 一定 要 做到。

❷ Sān cì bānjiā de mǔqīn
三 次 搬家 的 母亲

Mèngzǐ shì Zhōngguó gǔdài yī gè hěn hǎo de lǎoshī. Xǔduō yǒumíng de rén dōu shì tā de xuésheng.
孟子 是 中国 古代 一 个 很 好 的 老师。许多 有名 的 人 都 是 他 的 学生。

Zài Mèngzǐ hěn xiǎo de shíhou, fùqīn jiù sǐ le. Tā yīzhí hé mǔqīn yīqǐ shēnghuó.
在 孟子 很 小 的 时候，父亲 就 死 了。他 一直 和 母亲 一起 生活。

Yī kāishǐ, tāmen zhù zài shùlín pángbiān. Mèngzǐ chángcháng gēn fùjìn de xiǎohái yīqǐ wán, bù ài dúshū.
一 开始，他们 住 在 树林 旁边。孟子 常常 跟 附近 的 小孩 一起 玩，不 爱 读书。

Mǔqīn kàndào le, jiù shuō: "Bù xíng, wǒ bù néng
母亲 看到 了，就 说：“不 行，我 不 能

ràng wǒ de háizi zhù zài
让 我 的 孩子 住 在

zhèlǐ
这里。”

Tā dài zhe Mèngzǐ bāndào
她 带 着 孟子 搬到

shìchǎng pángbiān shēnghuó
市场 旁边 生活 。

Bùjiǔ Mèngzǐ jiù hé fùjìn
不久，孟子 就 和 附近

de xiǎohái yīqǐ gēn shāngrén
的 小孩 一起 跟 商人

xuéxí zuò shēngyi
学习 做 生意。

Mencius

Mǔqīn kàndào le yòu shuō Zhège dìfang yě bù
母亲 看到 了，又 说：“这个 地方 也 不

shìhé wǒmen
适合 我们。”

Zhè yī cì tāmen bāndào xuéxiào fùjìn Xuéxiào de
这 一 次，他们 搬到 学校 附近。学校 的

lǎoshī hé xuésheng měitiān dōu huì lǐmào de hùxiāng wènhòu
老师 和 学生 每天 都 会 礼貌 地 互相 问候。

Mèngzǐ kàndào zhīhòu jiù jìzhu yě xué tāmen zhèyàng zuò
孟子 看到 之后 就 记住，也 学 他们 这样 做。

Mǔqīn kàndào le jiù gāoxìng de shuō Zhèlǐ cáishì
母亲 看到 了，就 高兴 地 说：“这里 才是

shìhé wǒmen shēnghuó de dìfang a
适合 我们 生活 的 地方 啊！”

Měi gè rén dōu huì shòudào huánjìng de yǐngxiǎng Yào háizi
每 个 人 都 会 受到 环境 的 影响。要 孩子

biàn hǎo jiùyào dào shìhé de dìfang shēnghuó
变 好，就要 到 适合 的 地方 生活。

Translation

❶ Sun Wu trains his troops

Sun Wu was a capable military strategist in ancient China.

On one occasion, he spoke to his king about training the army. The king wanted to test his ability to command, and so he wanted Sun to train a company of female soldiers.

Sun chose a hundred ordinary ladies, and appointed two of the king's concubines as the company commanders.

Upon commencing the training, Sun told these ladies: "You are now soldiers and must follow orders. Those who do not obey orders will be punished."

Sun gave an order, but none of the ladies did what he said.

Sun repeated his order, and asked the two company commanders to lead by example. But the two concubines only stood there giggling, as if they did not hear him.

Sun told these ladies: "Although the two company commanders are the king's concubines, they did not obey orders, and so they must be punished."

With these words, Sun gave orders to have the two concubines killed.

The ladies were terrified. They immediately obeyed Sun's orders and put their heart into training. A few months later, these ladies had become real soldiers.

It is said that Sun Wu did not speak much when training his troops. But when he did, he was sure to keep to his word.

❷ The mother who moved house three times

Mencius was a fine teacher in ancient China. Many famous people were his students.

When Mencius was very young, after his father passed away, Mencius lived with his mother.

At first they lived next to a forest. Mencius would play with the neighboring kids there instead of studying.

When his mother saw this, she said: "No, I cannot let my child stay here."

She brought Mencius to live next to a market. Soon after, Mencius and the neighboring kids were learning how to do business from the merchants there.

When Mencius' mother saw what was happening, she said: "This place is not suitable for us."

Finally, they moved nearby a school. The teachers and students in the school would greet one another politely every day. When Mencius saw this, he remembered their actions and learned to do the same.

When Mencius' mother observed her son's behaviour, she said happily: "Now this is a suitable place for us to live!"

Every person is influenced by their environment. To change one's children for the better, one must find a suitable place for them to live.

Expansion Reading

The Chinese way of teaching and learning

In China, teachers and students alike are influenced by two thousand years of traditional Chinese philosophy of education, especially the ideas of Confucius.

Confucius' philosophy of education advocates *yincaishijiao* (因材施教), which means to teach students according to their ability. Teachers should take into account the unique situation of each individual student when coaching them. Today, with the growing population of China, there are many students in every class. Although it is not easy for teachers to make allowances for every student, they try to reveal to every student their strengths and weaknesses through reviewing assignments, individual counseling, performance appraisals and other methods to help students improve. Teachers also make use of their students' feedback to constantly improve the quality of their teaching.

The saying *zunshizhongdao*（尊师重道）means to honor teachers and respect knowledge. Since ancient times, teachers have held high social status in China. People are always willing to listen to their opinions. September 11 is Teacher's Day in China. On this day, students who are still in school, as well as those who have graduated, will send their teachers flowers and cards as a tribute to their tireless dedication.

The saying *jiaoxuexiangzhang*（教学相长）sums up the relationship between teaching and learning in China. Teachers put their hearts into educating students, students respect teachers, and the process of teaching and learning enables both teachers and students to mutually develop and improve one another.

GAMES FOR FUN

Which of the scenes shown below are related to education in China?

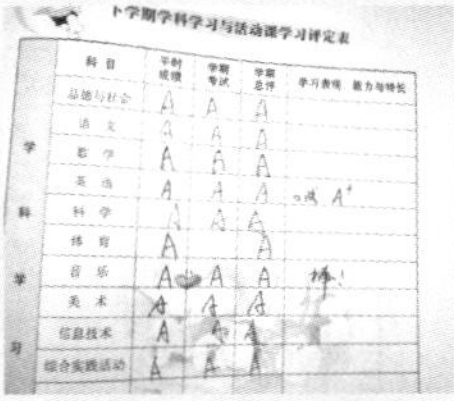

(a)

(b)

(c)

(d)

(e)

Answer: A, B, D

Shēnghuó de zhìhuì

生活的智慧

Wisdom in everyday life

Pre-reading Questions

1. Try to recall the most recent problem you encountered in your daily life. How did you resolve it?
2. Do you have a goal that you are unable to complete? Try breaking it down into smaller parts, and see if you can complete these one by one.

Bǎ niú jiàozuò bàba

❶ 把牛叫做“爸爸”

Yī gè fùqīn hé érzi zhù zài shānshang měitiān dōu yào gǎn zhe niú dào shānxià mài dōngxi. Fùqīn fùzé gǎn niú, érzi fùzé kàn lù.

一个父亲和儿子住在山上，每天都要赶着牛到山下卖东西。父亲负责赶牛，儿子负责看路。

Lùshang yǒu hěn duō wān, měicì kàndào wānlù de shíhou, érzi jiù huì jiào: "Bàba, qiánmian yǒu wānlù a!"

路上有很多弯，每次看到弯路的时候，儿子就会叫：“爸爸，前面有弯路啊！”

Yǒu yī cì fùqīn bìng le érzi yī gè rén gǎnniú
有一次，父亲病了，儿子一个人赶牛

dào shānxià qù
到山下去。

Dào le wānlù qián niú jiù tíng le xiàlái Érzi yòng
到了弯路前，牛就停了下来。儿子用

le hěn duō bànfǎ niú háishi bù yuànyì xiàng qián zǒu
了很多办法，牛还是不愿意向前走。

Zuìhòu érzi juédìng shǐyòng píngshí de zuòfǎ Tā
最后，儿子决定使用平时的做法。他

kàojìn niú de shēnbiān dàshēng de hǎn Bàba qiánmian
靠近牛的身边，大声地喊：“爸爸，前面

yǒu wānlù a
有弯路啊！”

Hǎn le zhè yī shēng niú guǒrán wǎng wānlù zǒu guoqu
喊了这一声，牛果然往弯路走过去

le
了。

Bùguǎn shì rén háishi dòngwù dōu yǒu xíguàn Hǎo de
不管是人还是动物，都有习惯。好的

xíguàn duō le rén de shēnghuó jiù huì hǎo qilai
习惯多了，人的生活就会好起来。

Fàngxia
❷ 放下

Yǒu yī gè shàonián xiǎng chéngwéi yī gè zhīshi hěn
有一个少年，想成为一个知识很

fēngfù de rén yúshì nǔlì de xuéxí
丰富的人，于是努力地学习。

Kěshì jǐ nián guòqù le tā juéde zìjǐ měi
可是，几年过去了，他觉得自己每

fāngmiàn dōu dǒng yīxiē dàn méiyǒu yī zhǒng bǐ biéren qiáng
方面都懂一些，但没有一种比别人强。

Shàonián hěn bù kāixīn jiù qù qǐngjiào lǎoshī
少年很不开心，就去请教老师。

Lǎoshī duì tā shuō Wǒmen qù páshān ba Dào le
老师对他说：“我们去爬山吧。到了

shān de zuì gāo chù nǐ jiù zhīdao gāi zěnyàng zuò le
山的最高处，你就知道该怎样做了。”

Lǎoshī dài zhe shàonián mànman zǒu shàng shān Yīlùshang
老师带着少年慢慢走上山。一路上，

tāmen kàndào hěn duō piàoliang de xiǎo shítou lǎoshī jiù ràng
他们看到很多漂亮的小石头，老师就让

shàonián bǎ tā xǐhuan de xiǎo shítou dōu shōu qilai
少年把他喜欢的小石头都收起来。

Hái méi zǒu dào yī bàn shàonián yǐjing ná zhe hěn duō
还没走到一半，少年已经拿着很多

xiǎo shítou Tā duì lǎoshī shuō Lǎoshī zhèxiē shítou
小石头。他对老师说：“老师，这些石头

hěn zhòng wǒ ná bù dòng le Wǒmen zhèyàngzi zěn kěyǐ
很重，我拿不动了。我们这样子怎可以

zǒu dào shān de zuì gāochù ne
走到山的最高处呢？”

Lǎoshī shuō Nàme nǐ
老师说：“那么你

gāi zěnme bàn ne
该怎么办呢？”

Shàonián shuō Wǒ xiǎng
少年说：“我想

wǒmen yīnggāi fàngxia yīxiē shítou
我们应该放下一些石头

a
啊！”

Lǎoshī xiào zhe diǎntóu
老师笑着点头。

Beautiful pebbles

Shàonián kàn zhe lǎoshī tūrán míngbai tā zhèyàng zuò de
少年看着老师，突然明白他这样做的

yuányīn le
原因了。

Méiyǒu yī gè rén nénggòu bǎ suǒyǒu shìqing dōu zuòdào zuì
没有一个人能够把所有事情都做到最

hǎo Yào chénggōng jiùyào xué huì fàngxia yīxiē bù bìyào de
好。要成功，就要学会放下一些不必要的

dōngxi
东西。

Hòulái shàonián zhuānmén qù xuéxí kēxué zhōngyú
后来，少年专门去学习科学，终于

chéngwéi le yī gè yǒumíng de kēxuéjiā
成为了一个有名的科学家。

Translation

❶ Calling an ox "father"

A father and son lived on a mountain. Every day they would take their ox down the mountain to buy things. The father would herd the ox, while the son would watch the road.

There were many bends in the road. Every time he saw a bend, the son would yell: "Father, there is a bend ahead!"

Once when the father fell ill, the son had to herd the ox down the mountain on his own.

Upon reaching a bend, the ox stopped. The son tried many ways, but still the ox would not move forward.

Finally, the son decided to do what he usually did. He leaned near the ox and yelled: "Father, there is a bend ahead!"

With this, the ox indeed walked towards the twisting road.

People and animals are both creatures of habit. Having good habits will help improve one's life.

❷ Learning to let go

There was a young man who wanted to be a knowledgeable person, and so he put a lot of effort into his studies.

A few years passed. He felt that although he knew a little bit of everything, he was not better than other people in any particular area.

The young man was not happy, and so he went to consult a teacher.

The teacher said to him: "Let's go climb a mountain. When you get to the highest point, you will know what to do."

The teacher took the young man slowly up the mountain. On their way up, they saw many beautiful stones. The teacher suggested the young man collect all the stones that he liked.

Even before they were halfway through their journey, the young man was already carrying many stones. He said to his teacher: "Teacher, these stones are very heavy. I can't carry them any further. How can we get to the highest point like this?"

The teacher said: "So what should you do?"

The young man said: "I think I should get rid of some stones!"

The teacher smiled and nodded his head.

The young man looked at his teacher, and suddenly he understood his reason for doing this.

No one can be good at everything. To be successful, one must learn to let go of things that are not needed.

The young man later committed himself to studying science, and eventually became a famous scientist.

Expansion Reading

Folk sayings: Documenting the wisdom of everyday life

Herbal tea with a bitter taste

Like other countries, China has many folk sayings of its own. These folk sayings embody the experience accumulated in everyday life, and represent the wisdom of common people.

The folk saying *kukouliangyao*（苦口良药）, means that the more bitter the medicine, the better it is for treating an illness. This is because Chinese medicine is made from various herbs, and the medicine made by boiling these herbs is usually bitter. Through practical long-term medical studies, people have discovered that medicine that is more bitter often works better in treating illnesses. This saying has become an appropriate summary of this observation.

Over time, this saying has become used to express the idea: Frank advice and sharp criticism may sound quite unbearable, but they are useful in correcting one's shortcomings and mistakes.

In China, you may also hear the saying *pianyimeihaohuo, haohuobupianyi*（便宜没好货，好货不便宜）, which means a quality product has its value, and will not come cheap. We can often hear parents using this saying to educate their children. A quality product will require quality machinery during production, quality workers to produce it, more care when transporting it, and all these will naturally increase the production cost. That is why the selling price of the product is higher in order to reflect its value, and for the businessman to make money.

Can you find more folk sayings from China that reflect the wisdom of everyday life?

GAMES FOR FUN

In everyday life, we often encounter food that are past their expiry date, such as milk. But expired milk can actually be very useful! How do you think it can be used?

(A)

(B)

(C)

(D)

Answer: A, B, D

Bù yīyàng de xuéxí

不一样的学习

A different approach to learning

Pre-reading Questions

1. When mastering a skill, what do you think one should be mindful of?
2. What do you think is the true meaning of a black belt?

Shèjiàn

❶ 射箭

Cóngqián yǒu yī gè rén gēn lǎoshī xuéxí shèjiàn
从前，有一个人跟老师学习射箭。

Tā de lǎoshī méiyǒu jiāo tā rènhé shèjiàn de dòngzuò zhǐ yāoqiú tā kàn zhe mùbiāo de shíhou yǎn bù néng dòng
他的老师没有教他任何射箭的动作，只要求他看着目标的时候，眼不能动。

Tā liànxí le liǎng nián zhōngyú zuòdào dāng tā kàn zhe mùbiāo shí yǒu dōngxi diào zài miànqián yǎn dōu bù dòng yī xià
他练习了两年，终于做到当他看着目标时，有东西掉在面前，眼都不动一下。

Zhīhòu lǎoshī yòu yāoqiú tā bǎ xiǎo dōngxi kàn de
之后，老师又要求他把小东西看得
hěn dà hěn qīngchu jiù xiàng nà dōngxi fàng zài yǎnqián
很大很清楚，就像那东西放在眼前
yīyàng
一样。

Tā liànxí le sān nián zhōngyú nénggòu bǎ hěn xiǎo de
他练习了三年，终于能够把很小的
chóngzi kàn de xiàng yuèliang yīyàng dà
虫子看得像月亮一样大。

Zhèshíhou tā de lǎoshī qǐng tā yòng jiàn shè xiàng
这时候，他的老师请他用箭射向
qiánmian yī kē shùshang de chóngzi Jiéguǒ zhège rén
前面一棵树上的虫子。结果，这个人
dì-yī cì shèjiàn jiù shèzhòng mùbiāo le
第一次射箭，就射中目标了。

Lǎoshī xiào zhe duì tā shuō Nǐ yǐjing dǒngde shèjiàn
老师笑着对他说：“你已经懂得射箭
le
了。”

Yuánlái yào xuéhǎo yī gè jìshù bìxū yào zhǎngwò zhu
原来，要学好一个技术，必须要掌握住
zuì zhòngyào de bùfen
最重要的部分。

Bow and arrows

Hēi dài de zhēnzhèng yìyì

❷ 黑带的真正意义

Zài yī jiā wǔshù xuéxiào li, yī gè xuésheng zhèngzài jiēshòu lǎoshī gěi tā de hēidài.

在一家武术学校里，一个学生正在接受老师给他的黑带。

Zhège xuésheng zài lǎoshī de zhǐdǎo xià, jīngguò duō nián de xùnliàn, zhōngyú zài wǔshù bǐsài zhōng qǔdé hǎo chéngjì.

这个学生在老师的指导下，经过多年的训练，终于在武术比赛中取得好成绩。

Zhège shíhou, lǎoshī duì xuésheng shuō: "Zài jiēshòu zhè tiáo hēidài zhīqián, nǐ yào huídá yī gè wèntí: Hēidài de zhēnzhèng yìyì shì shénme?"

这个时候，老师对学生说："在接受这条黑带之前，你要回答一个问题：黑带的真正意义是什么？"

Xuésheng shuō: "Hēidài dàibiǎo wǒ de xùnliàn kěyǐ jiéshù le."

学生说："黑带代表我的训练可以结束了。"

Lǎoshī tīng le tā de huídá, méiyǒu shuōhuà.

老师听了他的回答，没有说话。

Xuésheng yòu shuō: "Hēidài shì wǒ rènzhēn liànxí de chéngguǒ."

学生又说："黑带是我认真练习的成果。"

Zhècì, lǎoshī duì tā shuō: "Nǐ hái méiyǒu zīgé qǔdé zhè tiáo hēidài, yī nián hòu zài lái ba."

这次，老师对他说："你还没有资格取得这条黑带，一年后再来吧。"

Yī nián zhīhòu xuésheng láidào lǎoshī miànqián lǎoshī
一年之后，学生来到老师面前，老师
yòu yī cì tíchū tóngyàng de wèntí
又一次提出同样的问题。

Xuésheng shuō Hēidài dàibiǎo zhe wǔshù de zuìgāo
学生说：“黑带代表着武术的最高
chéngjiù
成就。”

Lǎoshī tīng le tā de huídá háishi ràng tā yī nián
老师听了他的回答，还是让他一年
hòu zài huílai
后再回来。

Yòu yī nián guòqù le xuésheng láidào lǎoshī miànqián
又一年过去了，学生来到老师面前，
lǎoshī réngrán tíchū nà yī tiáo wèntí
老师仍然提出那一条问题。

Xuésheng zhèyàng huídá Hēidài dàibiǎo wǒ de nénglì
学生这样回答：“黑带代表我的能力
réngrán bù zúgòu xūyào gèng gāo de yāoqiú hé gèng duō
仍然不足够，需要更高的要求和更多
de xùnliàn
的训练。”

Zhè yī cì lǎoshī
这一次，老师
xiào zhe duì tā shuō
笑着对他说：
Nǐ yǒu zīgé qǔdé
“你有资格取得
zhè tiáo hēidài le
这条黑带了。”

Black belt

Translation

❶ Shooting an arrow

A long time ago, there was a person who was learning archery from a teacher.

His teacher did not demonstrate any of the movements required to shoot an arrow, but only explained that when he looked at the target, his eyes must not wander.

He practiced for two years and finally achieved the skill. When he was looking at the target, an object could drop in front of him, and his eyes would not move even a bit.

After that, the teacher asked him to look at tiny objects as though they were big and clear, as if they were placed right before his eyes.

He practiced for three years, and finally he was able to look at a tiny insect as if it were as big as the Moon.

At this point, his teacher asked him to shoot an arrow at an insect on a tree. He shot his first arrow and hit the target.

The teacher smiled and said to him: "Now you know how to shoot an arrow."

It turns out that in order to learn a skill, one must grasp the most important parts.

❷ The true meaning of a black belt

In a martial arts school, a student was receiving his black belt from his teacher.

This student had trained for many years under the guidance of his teacher, and finally achieved good results in martial arts competitions.

The teacher said to the student: "Before accepting this black belt, you must answer this question: 'What is the true meaning of a black belt?'"

The student said: "The black belt means my training is finished."

The teacher heard his reply, but did not say anything.

The student then said: "The black belt is my reward for training hard."

This time, the teacher said to him: "You are still not qualified to receive this black belt. Come back in one year."

One year later, the student came before the teacher, and the teacher again asked the same question.

The student said: "The black belt represents the highest accomplishment in martial arts."

The teacher heard his reply, and again asked him to come back in one more year.

Another year passed. The student came before the teacher, and the teacher still asked the same question.

The student answered: "The black belt means my ability is still not adequate, and that I need to seek higher standards and even more training."

This time, the teacher smiled at him and said: "Now you are qualified to receive this black belt."

Expansion Reading

Is it really useful to do well in school?

Does one need to be good at studying? Throughout the ages, Chinese people have held different views.

Since the introduction of the imperial examination system in China, there has been a notion that "everything else is inferior, only studying is important", which means studying hard is more important than anything else. People thought that if a person did well in his studies, he could pass the state examinations, become a court official, and obtain the right to participate in state affairs. This was the best future that one could have.

Thus everyone, regardless of whether they were rich, poor, businessmen, farmers or officials, would send their children to school.

And the students, in order to pass examinations, would work hard at their studies, and would keep taking the national examinations until they passed.
Today, Chinese people no longer regard studying as the only path to a bright future. People no longer find it most desirable to be a statesman. Many people are not good at studying, but they are wealthy and lead comfortable lives. They stay in fine houses, have luxury cars, enjoy good food, and can easily travel to anywhere they wish. That is why, for a period of time, there emerged a notion that "studying is useless". To many people, it does not matter how well one does in his studies, as it is more important to know how to make money.
Many people feel that, as everyone has their own preferred lifestyle, the future they desire will be different. So long as a person can be useful to society, and is able to provide a good life for himself and his family, it does not really matter whether he is good in his studies. What do you think?

GAMES FOR FUN

There are many tools that can aid one in learning. Can you guess how students in ancient China used the tools shown below?

1. To help one in calculations
2. To help one in writing
3. To help remind one of the rules

Zhōngguó gǔdài de zhìhuì

中国古代的智慧

Ancient Chinese wisdom

Pre-reading Questions

1. Can you forgive your enemies? Why?
2. When you need to resolve an argument as a mediator, what would you do?

Bù jìzhu biéren de cuòwù

❶ 不 记住 别人 的 错误

Cóngqián yǒu yī gè guānyuán biéren zuò le duì tā bù
从前 有 一 个 官员，别人 做 了 对 他 不

hǎo de shìqing tā zǒng bù fàng zài xīnli
好 的 事情，他 总 不 放 在 心里。

Yǒu yī cì tā dào zhèngfǔ bàngōngshì de shíhou
有 一 次，他 到 政府 办公室 的 时候，

tīngdào yǒurén zài bèihòu pīpíng tā Tā méi shénme
听到 有人 在 背后 批评 他："他 没 什么

běnshi zěn kěyǐ dāng zhèyàng zhòngyào de guān ne
本事，怎 可以 当 这样 重要 的 官 呢？"

Zhège guānyuán jiù xiàng méi tīngjiàn yīyàng zǒujìn le
这个 官员 就 像 没 听见 一样，走进 了

bàngōngshì
办公室。

Kěshì tā shēnbiān de guānyuán tīngdào le dōu juéde
可是，他身边的官员听到了，都觉得
zhège pīpíng bù duì xiǎng bǎ shuōhuà de rén zhǎo chulai
这个批评不对，想把说话的人找出来。
Zhège guānyuán zhīdao hòu mǎshàng duì tāmen shuō Bù yào
这个官员知道后，马上对他们说："不要
qù bù yào qù
去，不要去。"

Qítā guānyuán hěn qíguài
其它官员很奇怪。

Tā shuō Rúguǒ wǒ zhīdao le nà yī gè rén de
他说："如果我知道了那一个人的
míngzi jiù bù huì wàngjì Zhèyàng wǒ zài gōngzuò de
名字，就不会忘记。这样，我在工作的
shíhou zǒng huì xiǎngqi tā céngjīng shuō guo wǒ de huàihuà zhè
时候总会想起他曾经说过我的坏话，这
duō bù hǎo a Qíshí
多不好啊！其实，
bù zhīdao nà yī gè
不知道那一个
rén de míngzi wǒ huì
人的名字，我会
shēnghuó de gèngjiā kuàilè
生活得更加快乐
ne
呢！"

Duì zìjǐ yāoqiú
对自己要求
duō yixiē duì biéren
多一些，对别人

An Officer of Ching Dynasty

yīnggāi shǎo yīxiē zhè jiùshì Zhōngguó gǔdài chuán xialai de
应该 少 一些，这 就是 中国 古代 传 下来 的

zhìhuì
智慧。

Duì yǔ cuò
❷ 对 与 错

Kǒngzǐ shì Zhōngguó gǔdài yī wèi wěidà de jiàoshī
孔子 是 中国 古代 一 位 伟大 的 教师。

Tā jiāo gěi xuésheng de dàoli yīzhí shì Zhōngguórén
他 教 给 学生 的 道理，一直 是 中国人

xuéxí gēncóng de biāozhǔn
学习、跟从 的 标准。

Yǒu yī cì tā de yī gè xuésheng dào jiēshang mǎi
有 一 次，他 的 一 个 学生 到 街上 买

dōngxi kàndào liǎng gè rén zài zhēng zhe shénme
东西，看到 两 个 人 在 争 着 什么。

Mài dōngxi de rén shuō Wǒ de bù yī chǐ yào sān
卖 东西 的 人 说：“我 的 布 一 尺 要 三

liǎng yínzi nǐ yào bā chǐ jiùshì èrshísì liǎng yínzi
两 银子，你 要 八 尺，就是 二十四 两 银子。

Shǎo yī liǎng wǒ dōu bù mài
少 一 两 我 都 不 卖！”

Mǎi dōngxi de rén shuō Yīnggāi shì èrshísān liǎng
买 东西 的 人 说：“应该 是 二十三 两，

nǐ yào èrshísì liǎng jiù bù duì
你 要 二十四 两 就 不 对。”

Kǒngzǐ de xuésheng yě bāng zhe mài dōngxi de rén Sān
孔子 的 学生 也 帮 着 卖 东西 的 人。三

gè rén zhēng le hěn jiǔ
个 人 争 了 很 久。

Kǒngzǐ de xuésheng shuō Rúguǒ wǒ cuò le wǒ
孔子 的 学生 说：“如果 我 错 了，我

jiù bǎ màozi gěi
就把帽子给
nǐ
你。”

Confucius

Mǎi dōngxi de
买东西的
rén hěn shēngqì jiù
人很生气，就
shuō Rúguǒ wǒ
说：“如果我
cuò le wǒ bǎ wǒ de tóu gěi nǐ
错了，我把我的头给你！”

Zuìhòu tāmen juédìng ràng Kǒngzǐ lái pànduàn shuí cáishì
最后，他们决定让孔子来判断谁才是
duì de
对的。

Kǒngzǐ tīng wán sān gè rén de huà xiào zhe duì xuésheng
孔子听完三个人的话，笑着对学生
shuō Nǐ cuò le kuài bǎ màozi gěi tā ba
说：“你错了，快把帽子给他吧。”

Mǎi dōngxi de rén hěn kāixīn ná zhe xuésheng de
买东西的人很开心，拿着学生的
màozi zǒu le
帽子走了。

Xuésheng bù míngbai Kǒngzǐ wèishénme zhèyàng zuò jiù
学生不明白孔子为什么这样做，就
wèn Lǎoshī nǐ zhīdao wǒ shì duì de wèishénme shuō
问：“老师，你知道我是对的，为什么说
wǒ cuò ne
我错呢？”

Kǒngzǐ shuō Nǐ shū le bǎ màozi gěi tā jiù
孔子说：“你输了，把帽子给他就

kěyǐ Kěshì nà yī gè rén shū le yào bǎ tā de
可以。可是那一个人输了，要把他的

tóu gěi nǐ a Yī jiàn shìqing de duìcuò zhòngyào háishi
头给你啊！一件事情的对错重要，还是

yī gè rén de shēngmìng zhòngyào ne Nǐ zuò zhè jiàn shì
一个人的生命重要呢？你做这件事

zhīqián yīnggāi rènzhēn de xiǎng qīngchu hòuguǒ a
之前，应该认真地想清楚后果啊！”

Translation

❶ Do not remember the faults of others

A long time ago, there was an official. When people did bad things to him, he never took it to heart.

On one occasion, when he was on his way to his office, he overheard somebody criticizing him behind his back: “He does not have much ability. How can he take on such an important post?”

The official acted as if he had not heard anything, and walked into his office.

But the officials beside him had heard it. They felt the criticism was unfair, and they wanted to go find the person who made those remarks.

When the official learned of this, he immediately told them: “Don’t go, don’t go.”

The other officials thought this was strange.

The official said: “If I know the person’s name, I will not forget it. So, while I am working, I will be recalling the bad things he said about me, and that will not be good! In fact, not knowing that person’s name will make me much happier!”

We should be more demanding of ourselves and less demanding of others. This is a piece of ancient Chinese wisdom that has passed down through the ages.

❷ Of right and wrong

Confucius was a great teacher in ancient China. The principles that he taught his students have always been the standards that Chinese people learn and adhere to.

On one occasion, one of his students went to the street to buy something, and saw two people arguing.

The seller said: "My cloth goes for two silver taels per foot. You want eight feet, which comes up to twenty-four taels. I will not sell for anything lower."

The buyer said: "It should be twenty-three taels. You are wrong to ask for twenty-four taels."

Confucius' student was on the side of the seller. The three people argued for a long time.

Confucius' student said: "If I am wrong, I will give you my hat."

The buyer was angry and said: "If I am wrong, I will give you my head!"

In the end, they decided to let Confucius determine who was right.

After listening to the three of them, Confucius smiled and said to his student: "You are wrong, so give him your hat."

The buyer was happy. He took the student's hat and left.

The student did not understand why Confucius did this. He asked: "Teacher, you know I was right, so why did you say I was wrong?"

Confucius said: "If you lost, you just had to give him your hat. But if that person lost, he would have had to give you his head! Which is more important – whether a matter is right or wrong, or a person's life? Before you did this, you should have seriously considered the consequences!"

Expansion Reading

Traditional virtues of China

China has been a country of etiquette since ancient times. Traditional virtues accumulated over two thousand years continue to influence the Chinese people today.

What are some of these traditional virtues?

One example is that the Chinese people attach great importance to personal relations, and they advocate treating relatives and friends with a kind heart. Chinese people are taught from a young age to be filial to their parents, and to cherish their siblings and friends. Hence, Chinese families tend to be very close-knit. Every year before the Chinese New Year, no matter how arduous the train ride is, thousands of migrant workers in cities across China insist on going back to their hometown for a reunion with their families. This demonstrates the importance of kinship in China.

The Chinese people also pay great attention to behavior in relationships. They believe that one should be modest, and there should be mutual respect when dealing with people. When referring to the shortcomings of other people, Chinese people often will not directly criticize them, but will get the message across in a subtle and tactful manner, in a way that is much easier for people to accept.

The Mid-bafumn Fastivat is a time for family reanions

In addition, Chinese people are concerned with benefiting society, and believe that individuals should conform to and serve the interests of society. When faced with calamities such as disasters and wars, Chinese people will often abandon their personal interests for the sake of their country and collective interests. This virtue was evident during events such as the snowstorms that hit southern China in 2008 and the massive Sichuan earthquake.

There are many other Chinese traditional virtues. Would you be interested to come to China and experience them for yourself?

Glossary

Common Words and Phrases			GCS Rank	Page
dài fu	大夫	doctor	1	*1*
zhuā	抓	seize	1	*2*
tiáo jiàn	条件	conditions	1	*3*
guān yuán	官员	official	2	*1*
duì dài	对待	deal with	1	*4*
gēn jù	根据	base on	1	*4*
cái liào	材料	materials	2	*9*
chóng zi	虫子	bug	2	*9*
guó wáng	国王	king	1	*10*
zuò zhàn	作战	fight	2	*16*
xiǎo tōu	小偷	thief	2	*16*
jūn duì	军队	troops	1	*16*
shù lín	树林	woodlands	1	*9*
zhàn chǎng	战场	battlefield	2	*18*
tóu fa	头发	hair	2	*23*
chú shī	厨师	chef	2	*23*
diào chá	调查	investigate	1	*24*
chéng rèn	承认	recognize	1	*23*
yā zi	鸭子	duck	2	*25*
shāng rén	商人	merchant	1	*25*
yǒu xiào	有效	effective	1	*4*
lián máng	连忙	promptly	1	*23*
gōng kāi	公开	open	1	*25*

GCS: HanBan / Confucius Institute Headquaters, The Graded Chinese Syllables, Characters and Words for the Application of Teaching Chinese to the Speakers of Other Languages, 2010.

kē	棵	numerary adjunct for trees	2	*32*
yuàn zi	院子	yard	1	*32*
jìng zi	镜子	mirror	2	*31*
jiāng jūn	将军	general	2	*16*
lǐ mào	礼貌	politeness	2	*38*
kàn bu qǐ	看不起	despise	2	*38*
zhì zào	制造	manufacture	1	*37*
zhàn dòu	战斗	combat	2	*38*
zì shā	自杀	suicide	2	*40*
ān pái	安排	arrange	1	*40*
tuō	脱	take off	2	*38*
shēn biān	身边	side	2	*31*
zhí wèi	职位	position	2	*47*
zhǔ dòng	主动	active	1	*47*
běn shi	本事	abilities	1	*45*
qiáng dà	强大	powerful	1	*45*
biǎo míng	表明	make clear	1	*47*
dài lǐng	带领	lead	1	*44*
yǒng gǎn	勇敢	brave	2	*44*
dāng zhōng	当中	among	1	*52*
zhòng shì	重视	pay attention to	1	*46*
xiāng zi	箱子	tank	2	*54*
dǒng de	懂得	understand	1	*18*
jì suàn	计算	calculate	1	*53*
mìng lìng	命令	command	2	*59*
chǔ fèn	处分	punishment	2	*59*
àn zhào	按照	according to	1	*59*

xùn liàn	训练	train	1	*58*
kǎo yàn	考验	test	1	*58*
chóng fù	重复	repeat	1	*59*
jūn rén	军人	soldier	1	*36*
lǐng dǎo	领导	leadership	1	*58*
bān	搬	move to	2	*60*
shì chǎng	市场	marketplace	1	*61*
wèn hòu	问候	send one's regards to	2	*61*
shēng yi	生意	business	1	*61*
wān	弯	curve	2	*65*
fēng fù	丰富	abundant	1	*66*
qǐng jiào	请教	consult	1	*67*
zhuān mén	专门	specially	1	*68*
màn man	慢慢	slowly	2	*67*
dòng zuò	动作	movement	1	*72*
shè jiàn	射箭	archery	2	*72*
chéng jiù	成就	achievements	1	*75*
zī gé	资格	qualifications	1	*74*
bèi hòu	背后	behind somebody's back	1	*79*
gǔ dài	古代	ancient	1	*8*
wěi dà	伟大	great	1	*81*
pàn duàn	判断	determine	1	*82*
biāo zhǔn	标准	standard	1	*81*
hòu guǒ	后果	consequence	1	*83*
mào zi	帽子	hat	2	*82*